Table of Contents

Chapter 1

Introduction and Overview

I. Introduction

A. Purpose and Intent of this Guide

This policy guide will assist correctional administrators, medical and mental health staff, training coordinators, line staff, and policymakers as they craft policies to address the treatment of lesbian, gay, bisexual, transgender, and intersex individuals (LGBTI) in custodial settings. It may also help agencies that are paying greater attention to the needs of LGBTI individuals as they work to implement the Prison Rape Elimination Act (PREA) standards, which require correctional agencies to safely screen, classify, and house lesbian,

> Meeting the needs and protecting the rights of LGBTI people in various custodial settings presents both challenges and opportunities for society's institutions, including law enforcement and corrections.

gay, bisexual, and transgender inmates as well as those who have intersex conditions. By integrating information about LGBTI individuals into policies, practices, and organizational culture, agencies will be better able to meet the needs of LGBTI inmates and increase the comfort level of staff who work with this population on a daily basis.

This guide includes information that will help adult correctional facilities and juvenile justice agencies to assess, develop, or improve policies and practices regarding LGBTI individuals in their custody. The guide is not meant to be a quick reference for writing policies appropriate for all agencies and/or facilities. It is intentionally vague on "how to" advice and "plug and play" policy guidance. Guides for writing policies exist in many forms.[1] Rather, the purpose of this guide is to (1) define agencies' obligations to LGBTI populations, both legally and in accordance with PREA standards, (2) begin a dialogue within agencies regarding the safety and treatment needs of LGBTI populations, and (3) guide agencies in asking good questions about practices and implementation strategies for meeting the needs of LGBTI populations.

Agencies need policies to address the treatment of LGBTI individuals in custodial settings to meet constitutional and other obligations to provide humane treatment to those in their custody. Additionally, strong policies can help mitigate the risk of liability to the agency and its staff in the event of an incident or litigation. Part of the mission for all correctional agencies is to provide safe and secure environments for all individuals in their care and custody. State and federal law imposes legal obligations on correctional and juvenile agencies for the treatment of all persons in custody, with specific provisions for LGBTI populations.

Chapter 1 of this policy guide discusses general terminology and the reasons why agencies need policies. It discusses the terminology necessary to understand issues of sexual orientation. Without a basic understanding of these terms, it is difficult to understand the issues and concerns of LGBTI individuals and the challenges they face in custodial settings. Additionally, understanding and proper use of terminology are at the core of developing policy and practice as they relate to LGBTI inmates and youth. In addition to this general discussion of terminology, there is a full glossary of terms in appendix A. It is important to remember that these terms are evolving and can vary depending on who is using them. However, the glossary is consistent with the PREA standards, and this set of definitions is used in this publication. Chapter 2 addresses the needs of juvenile justice agencies in creating policies for LGBTI youth in custody. Chapter 3 discusses the needs of adult correctional settings (prisons, jails, and community corrections facilities) in developing LGBTI policies for inmates or residents. The appendixes include a glossary; a case law digest; resources addressing LGBTI issues along with resources for LGBTI youth and adults; sample policies for prisons, jails, community corrections, and juvenile agencies; and a training matrix.

B. Issues in Providing Care and Safety for LGBTI Individuals in Custody

During the past three decades, an increasing number of individuals have openly identified as lesbian, gay, bisexual, or transgender, and many young people are actively questioning their sexual orientation and gender identity. In addition, society has developed an increased awareness of people living with intersex conditions. Today, individuals who are—or are perceived to be—LGBTI are a part of nearly all segments of society, including those who are inmates and staff in correctional settings. Given the unique circumstance of LGBTI people under the jurisdiction of both adult and juvenile criminal justice systems, as well as those who are housed in immigration detention, correctional authorities must be able to ensure that LGBTI people in their custody will be safe.

In 2011, there was considerable change in legislative and policy decisions concerning LGBTI issues. Bullying initiatives, such as the It Gets Better campaign, have raised public awareness about the struggles of LGBTI youth.[2] School administrators responded in turn, displaying a heightened sensitivity toward LGBTI youth.[3] Schools enacted zero-tolerance policies and other antibullying measures aimed at eradicating violence and aggression toward LGBTI or other gender-nonconforming students.[4] Same-sex marriage advocates cheered the Obama administration's decision to no longer defend Defense of Marriage Act cases.[5] During the 2012 election season, voters were challenged to expand LGBTI rights, and they rose to the task—Maine, Maryland, and Washington joined Connecticut, Iowa, Massachusetts, New Hampshire, New York, Vermont, and the District of Columbia in approving same-sex marriages.[6] Furthermore, Minnesota residents rejected a ballot measure to amend the state constitution to define marriage as a union between a man and a woman.[7] Lastly, Wisconsin voters elected Tammy Baldwin as the first openly gay U.S. senator.[8]

Unfortunately, a lack of knowledge about LGBTI people, coupled with little guidance for correctional institutions on how to maintain safety and respectfully communicate with this population, has resulted in significant challenges for LGBTI people held in custodial settings. The nature and severity of these problems were at the forefront of PREA's enactment, the proposed standards developed by the National Prison Rape Elimination Commission (NPREC), and the final standards issued by the Department of Justice.

The following challenges were identified during the 2007 meeting:

- Lack of training in gender identity.

- Lack of a common language to refer to LGBTI individuals.

- Organizational culture issues.

- Lack of training in classification and housing of LGBTI individuals.

- Lack of appropriate housing options for LGBTI individuals.

- Lack of policies and procedures for how to treat LGBTI individuals from arrest through custody.

- Lack of experience in addressing the medical and mental healthcare needs of LGBTI individuals.

- Lack of services for LGBTI persons in custody and upon release.

In April 2007, the Center for Innovative Public Policies, Inc., through an initiative with the National Institute of Corrections (NIC), collaborated with The Project on Addressing Prison Rape to sponsor the meeting "Working with Lesbian, Gay, Bisexual, Transgender, and Intersex Populations in Corrections Systems: Identification of Issues and Resources, Development of Recommendations."[9] The meeting brought together a diverse group of stakeholders, subject-matter experts, and corrections officials to identify challenges, propose solutions, develop recommendations, and identify resources for agencies with LGBTI populations.

During the meeting, the group identified approximately 30 separate challenges; the resulting unpublished report also made a number of important recommendations for improving the treatment of LGBTI adults and youth in custody.

A primary recommendation was to develop a policy guide for correctional agencies on the issue. The concept of this policy guide was born from that recommendation; the guide seeks to address the needs identified during the 2007 meeting by providing policy and practice recommendations that will help correctional staff when working with LGBTI adults and youth in custody.

II. Evolving Terminology and Definitions

To be able to address the needs of LGBTI individuals in custodial settings, it is necessary to have a full understanding of the basic and appropriate terms that individuals use to present themselves. The most basic concepts are "sexual orientation" and "gender identity."

A. Gender Identity

Gender identity is a person's internal, deeply felt sense of being male or female, distinct from his or her sexual orientation. Everyone has a gender identity and, for many, their gender identity is consistent with their assigned sex at birth and their physical anatomy.

A **transgender** or **transsexual** person has a gender identity that is different from his/her assigned sex at birth. A transgender woman is a person whose birth sex is male but who understands herself to be, and desires to live her life as, a female; a transgender man is a person whose birth sex is female but who understands himself to be, and desires to live his life as, a male. A transgender person may publicly express his/her gender identity while very young, middle aged, or even elderly. **Transition** is the term that is often used to describe the time period when transgender people start publicly living their lives in accordance with their gender identity. Transition often includes a change in dress, hairstyle, and physical appearance; the use of a new name; and a change in pronoun (from "he" to "she," or vice versa). During transition, many transgender people will also begin to undergo medical treatments (such as hormone therapy or surgery) to change their physical bodies to better match their gender identity; however, not all transgender people undergo medical treatments.

Some people's gender-related appearance, characteristics, and behaviors—**gender expression**—cross genders or include aspects of both masculinity and femininity. The term **gender nonconforming** can be used to describe people whose gender expression is outside of societal assumptions for how men and women are expected to behave or appear.

Many transgender people experience high levels of distress that result in depression, anxiety, low self-esteem, and even suicide ideation.[10] For some, the high level of distress develops into a condition known as either **gender identity disorder (GID)** or **gender dysphoria**.[11] In 2012, the American Psychiatric Association (APA) announced its intention to remove the term "GID" from the forthcoming *Diagnostic and Statistical Manual of Mental Disorders, Fifth Edition,* and replace it with gender dysphoria.[12] The term "gender dysphoria" is used in this guide, except in circumstances where specific court holdings have turned on a GID diagnosis.

> Heterosexual people who are gender nonconforming, or do not conform to gender stereotypes, are often perceived by others to be LGBTI and face many of the same risks of maltreatment in custodial settings as LGBTI people do.

B. Sexual Orientation

Sexual orientation refers to a person's romantic and physical attraction to members of the same sex or a different sex. A continuum of sexual orientation exists, from exclusively heterosexual or "straight" (attraction to members of a different sex) to exclusively homosexual or "gay" or "lesbian" (attraction to members of the same sex), along with degrees of bisexuality (attraction to same-sex and different-sex people). People who are not sexually attracted to anyone are **asexual.** An asexual individual can still experience relationships but may not have feelings of sexual attraction or the desire to act on these feelings if they do occur.

C. Intersex

People who are **intersex** or have intersex conditions[13] are born with external genitalia, internal reproductive organs, chromosome patterns, and/or endocrine systems that do not fit typical definitions of male or female. The medical conditions causing these variations are sometimes grouped under the terms "intersex" or disorders of sex development.[14] It is estimated that 1 in 2,000 babies is born with an intersex condition.[15] Although most people with intersex conditions do not identify as transgender, because of their unique bodies or their gender expressions many experience abuse and harassment in correctional settings similar to the type of abuse transgender people experience.

D. Use of Terminology and Acronyms

Often, acronyms are used to refer to individuals who are "sexual minorities." The most common acronym is **LGBT**—lesbian, gay, bisexual, and transgender—and is often used to identify the full community of individuals who do not consider themselves heterosexual or who are transgender.

Some people also use **"Q"** to include individuals who self-identify as "queer" and/or "questioning." The term **questioning** refers to the active process in which young people explore their sexual orientation and/ or gender identity and question the societal assumption that they are heterosexual and/or gender conforming. Many LGBT people go through this process of questioning before "coming out" (or telling other people that they identify as LGBT). It is important to note that not all people who are questioning, especially young people, will later identify as LGBT.

The PREA standards do not use an acronym, but instead use the terms gay, lesbian, bisexual, transgender, and intersex.[16] The PREA standards also use the term "gender nonconforming" to encompass "any person whose appearance or manner does not conform to traditional societal gender expectations."[17]

> The American Counseling Association "opposes the promotion of 'reparative' therapy as a cure for individuals who are homosexual." The American Psychoanalytic Association believes that "[p]sychoanalytic technique does not encompass purposeful efforts to 'convert' or 'repair' an individual's sexual orientation."
>
> Whitman, Joy S., Harriet L. Glosoff, Michael M. Kocet, and Vilia Tarvydas. 2006. "Exploring Ethical Issues Related to Conversion or Reparative Therapy." *Counseling Today.*

In this guide, the acronym **LGBTI** is used to refer to the whole community of people who are sexual and gender minorities—lesbian, gay, bisexual, transgender, and intersex individuals. Additionally, the acronym **LGBTQI** (lesbian, gay, bisexual, transgender, questioning, and intersex) is used in chapter 2 of this guide to reflect the process of questioning that often occurs in adolescence.

III. Core Principles for Understanding LGBTI Individuals in Custody

Just as corrections officials must develop an understanding of core terms used by LGBTI people, there are also core principles that can help officials better understand sexual orientation and gender identity. These core principles are based on well-developed research and positions developed by medical and mental health professionals.

A. Awareness and Self-Identification

Research in the area of adolescent development demonstrates that both sexual orientation and gender identity are established at a very early age.[18] The latest research shows that children are disclosing their sexual orientation to others at younger ages than in previous generations.[19] Not all youth who have same-sex attractions, experiences, or relationships self-identify as lesbian, gay, or bisexual.[20] For some, it can take many years to understand and become comfortable with their identities, and some people do not come out until much later in their lives.[21]

B. Do No Harm: The Necessity of Medical and Mental Health Care

Health professionals agree that a person's gender identity is an ingrained and inherent part of his/her overall identity, and attempts to change it will be ineffective and could potentially cause significant harm.[22] Even though some people may choose not to act on their feelings or do not self-identify as lesbian, gay, or bisexual, individuals with same-sex attractions cannot change their sexual orientation.[23]

> **MYTH:** Being LGBTI makes a person more likely to commit a sexual offense.
>
> **FACT:** Research confirms that there is no connection between an individual's sexual orientation and his/her propensity to commit a sexual offense.
>
> Herek, Gregory M., "Facts About Homosexuality and Child Molestation," http://psychology.ucdavis.edu/rainbow/html/facts_molestation.html; Goldman, Linda. 2008. *Coming Out, Coming In: Nurturing the Well-Being and Inclusion of Gay Youth in Mainstream Society.* Routledge, pp. 42–43; McConaghy, Nathanial. 1998. "Paedophelia: A Review of the Evidence." *Australian and New Zealand Journal of Psychiatry* 32:252, 259–60; Jenny, Carole, Thomas A. Roesler, and Kimberly L. Poyer. 1994. "Are Children at Risk for Sexual Abuse by Homosexuals?" *Pediatrics* 94(1):41–44.

Objective scientific research demonstrates that lesbian, gay, and bisexual identities fall within the range of normal sexual development and are not associated with mental disorders or emotional or social problems,[24] and they are not the result of prior sexual abuse or any other trauma.[25] In addition, numerous studies over the past 20 years have found that transgender individuals do not have serious underlying psychopathologies that cause or influence their transgender identities and that the number of transgender people with reported psychiatric problems mirrors that in the general population.[26]

The World Professional Association for Transgender Health (WPATH)[27] has issued internationally accepted protocols for the treatment of youth and adults with gender dysphoria.[28] Treatment focuses on supporting a person's understanding of his/her gender and is highly personalized, based on individual needs.[29] Treatment can include a combination of counseling, hormone therapy, and/or surgeries as well as encouraging gender expression and gender identification.[30] Disrespecting, punishing, or prohibiting transgender people from expressing their gender identity can lead to depression, suicide attempts, and problems with relationships, school, and work.[31]

Medical experts do not view transitional treatments for transgender people as dangerous or experimental.[32] Both the American Medical Association and the APA agree that these transition-related treatments are effective and medically necessary for individuals who have been appropriately evaluated.[33] Medical organizations further recognize and support the need for transgender-specific care in custodial settings.[34]

IV. Emerging Data on LGBTI Individuals in Custodial Settings and the Challenges They Face

Individuals who are (or who are perceived to be) LGBTI are a presence in jails, prisons, juvenile facilities, community corrections facilities, and immigration detention facilities. A 2008 study conducted by the Bureau of Justice Statistics (BJS) found that 8 percent of the prison inmates surveyed identified a sexuality other than heterosexual (114,300 out of 1,430,300 surveyed inmates of federal and state prisons).[35] Recently, a BJS survey of juvenile facilities found that more than 12 percent of youth self-identified as nonheterosexual.[36]

A. LGBTI Individuals in Custodial Settings

LGBTI individuals are at significant risk for contact with the justice or correctional system. Although the social climate for LGBTI people has improved significantly over the past few decades, LGBTI youth and adults continue to face hostility and discrimination in their homes, schools, workplaces, communities, and social service settings. As a result, LGBTI people may not have access to support networks to help prevent entrance into the criminal justice system.

> The National Commission on Correctional Health Care (NCCHC) adopted a position statement that provides guidance to health professionals working in correctional settings about their responsibility to ensure the physical and mental health of transgender people in custody. According to NCCHC, the proper approach to transgender medical care is to follow the World Professional Association for Transgender Health Standards of Care, ensuring that transgender people living in institutional settings have access to the same medical treatments that would be available to them in the community.
>
> National Commission on Correctional Health Care, Position Statement on Transgender Health Care in Correctional Settings, October 18, 2009, http://www.ncchc.org/transgender-health-care-in-correctional-settings.

Studies of LGBTI youth in school settings reveal that they experience a higher frequency of verbal harassment and physical assault than their heterosexual counterparts.[37] Reports of physical violence include individuals' clothes being forcibly removed, gang rape,[38] and even death.[39] LGBTI youth often face these challenges not only at school but also in their homes and communities.[40] Family rejection and school failure can lead to other problems, including homelessness,[41] involvement in the sex industry,[42] psychological problems,[43] and self-medication with alcohol and drugs.[44] Consequently, LGBTI people may have disproportionate contact with the criminal justice system that may begin, for some, in adolescence and continue into adulthood.[45]

Furthermore, LGBTI identity can sometimes overwhelm companion issues of poverty and race. A study conducted by the National Gay and Lesbian Task Force and the National Center for Transgender Equality found that transgender individuals were four times more likely to live in extreme poverty.[46] Individuals living in poverty have a substantially higher rate of involvement with the juvenile and criminal justice systems. These issues are exacerbated for LGBTI people of color, who are already disproportionately poor and may be detained by law enforcement because of their race.[47]

B. What the Data Illustrate

LGBTI individuals who have contact with the juvenile or adult justice system often experience a number of serious challenges that begin at arrest and continue through release. These issues include abusive and demeaning contact with criminal justice officials; being inappropriately classified and housed; lack of access to resources, including medical and mental health care; and abusive treatment (verbal, emotional, physical, and sexual) from other inmates and staff.

Recent research efforts have focused on the incidence of sexual violence against LGBTI individuals in custody. Research and testimony about the vulnerability of those who are, or are perceived to be, LGBTI animated the passage of PREA in 2003. Even prior to PREA's passage, research on sexual abuse in correctional facilities consistently documented that men and women with nonheterosexual orientations, transgender individuals, and people with intersex conditions were highly vulnerable to sexual abuse.[48]

The NPREC proposed standards to address prison rape on June 23, 2009;[49] compliance indicators were included to address the specific vulnerability of LGBTI populations based on the finding that "certain individuals are more at risk of sexual abuse than others."[50] In particular, the NPREC found that "corrections administrators need to do more to identify those who are vulnerable and protect them in ways that do not leave them isolated and without access to rehabilitative programming."[51]

Research conducted by BJS pursuant to its mandate under PREA supports the NPREC's findings and earlier research on the prevalence of sexual abuse in custodial settings.[52] The BJS survey of youth in juvenile facilities found that more than 1 in 5 nonheterosexual youth reported sexual victimization involving another youth or a facility staff member, whereas slightly more than 1 in 10 heterosexual youth reported sexual victimization.[53] The same study found that nonheterosexual youth were almost 10 times more likely than heterosexual youth to report they had been sexually abused by other youth while in custody (12.5 percent and 1.3 percent, respectively).

A 2008 BJS study of federal and state prisoners found that among 1,316,000 heterosexual inmates, only 1.3 percent reported sexual victimization at the hands of another inmate and 2.5 percent reported victimization by a staff member.[54] Among 114,300 inmates with a nonheterosexual orientation, 11.2 percent reported sexual victimization perpetrated by another inmate and 6.6 percent reported sexual victimization by a staff member.[55]

> In matters of housing, recreation, and work assignments, custody staff should be aware that transgender people are common targets for violence. Accordingly, appropriate safety measures should be taken regardless of whether the person is placed in male or female housing areas.
>
> National Commission on Correctional Health Care, Position Statement on Transgender Health Care in Correctional Settings, October 18, 2009, available at http://www.ncchc.org/transgender-health-care-in-correctional-settings.

> A number of successful lawsuits have been filed by transgender inmates against the Federal Bureau of Prisons, state departments of corrections, and local jails across the country. In recent years, federal courts have issued decisions in every circuit as well as the U.S. Supreme Court. These cases involve allegations of inadequate health care, deliberate indifference to abuse, and other forms of mistreatment.
>
> De'Lonta v. Johnson, 708 F.3d 520 (4th Cir. 2013).

Other data illustrate that transgender women and girls are highly vulnerable to sexual abuse, especially when housed in facilities for men or boys.[56] The University of California's Center for Evidence-Based Corrections found that "[s]exual assault is *13 times* more prevalent among transgender inmates, with 59 percent reporting being sexually assaulted."[57] In this study, transgender victims were also far more likely than other victims to have been sexually assaulted on multiple occasions.[58] Such findings make clear that "[e]ven when compared to other relatively vulnerable populations, transgender people are perilously situated."[59] Because of this concern, the American Psychological Association and the National Commission on Correctional Health Care have both issued statements recognizing that transgender inmates are at especially high risk of abuse and calling for their protection.[60]

C. Risk, Housing, and Classification

Because there are no specific policies to provide guidance for correctional staff on exercising appropriate judgment for risk assessment and placement of LGBTI inmates, these inmates are most often placed or housed according to their genitalia or assigned sex at birth. If an independent medical analysis and risk assessment are not conducted, inmates' safety, security, or programming needs may be at risk; this also risks the safety and security of other inmates and staff.[61] This is an issue in both adult and juvenile settings, where LGBTI youth can face denial of access to health care, inappropriate housing, and punishment for expressing their gender.[62]

Placement based on biology particularly impacts transgender women placed in men's facilities. The NPREC found that transgender women housed with men are "at extremely high risk for abuse."[63] These women report verbal harassment, abusive strip searches, sexual assault, long-term administrative detention, and denials of program participation.[64] The NPREC found that "research on sexual abuse in correctional facilities consistently documents the vulnerability of ... transgender individuals."[65] LGBTI inmates also report that agency staff single out transgender people for abuse and have ignored or encouraged abuse by other inmates.[66] Although little research exists on inmates with intersex conditions, NPREC findings show that this group is vulnerable to sexual abuse.[67] PREA regulations incorporate special measures to protect both transgender and intersex inmates.[68] When individuals enter custody, authorities must make important decisions about risk, housing, and classification; these decisions are often made on the basis of gender. Because LGBTI inmates are gender nonconforming, this presents challenges at the outset.

Corrections officials are aware of the particular vulnerabilities LGBTI individuals face; many facilities house LGBTI populations in administrative segregation or special population units.[69] These options, although often based on a desire to protect vulnerable inmates from sexual harassment or assault, are effective for brief periods of time but have proven unworkable for a myriad of reasons. The PREA standards provide that "[i]nmates at high risk for sexual victimization shall not be placed in involuntary segregated housing unless an assessment of all available alternatives has been made, and a determination has been made that there is no available alternative means of separation from likely abusers."[70]

Administrative segregation, and the ensuing isolation from the general population for purposes of "safety," often exacerbates mental health conditions such as depression or gender dysphoria. In addition, isolation from the general population often means limited or no access to programming, regular visitation, or health care, all of which are necessary for LGBTI populations. Likewise, data suggest that special population units (such as those on Rikers Island and the San Francisco County Jail) have not kept inmates who identify as LGBTI any safer.[71]

LGBTQI youth have experiences that are similar to their adult counterparts. A study by the Equity Project documented the experiences of LGBTQI youth, finding that these youth in juvenile justice facilities were often labeled sexual predators, isolated from other youth, singled out, or even sent to sex offender programs. Youth were also denied access to education or group activities because staff lacked the capacity and skills to protect them from serious acts of physical, sexual, or verbal abuse.[72] LGBTQI youth were often placed in protective custody or administrative segregation, where they were confined to their cells for up to 23 hours a day.[73] These experiences and conditions put LGBTQI youth at risk for other mental health issues such as depression, low self-esteem, substance abuse, and suicide.[74]

> Based on their actual or perceived sexual orientation and gender identity, LGBTQI youth may be subjected to physical, sexual, and emotional abuse at the hands of other youth as well as facility staff members.
>
> Staff may treat LGBTQI youth disrespectfully and unfairly, or they may punish and ridicule youth because of their actual or perceived sexual orientation or gender identity.
>
> LGBTQI youth may also be segregated as a means of protecting them from abuse or based on an unfounded fear that they will prey on others in a sexual manner.
>
> National Sexual Violence Resource Center. 2009. *National Prison Rape Elimination Commission Report.* Washington, DC: National Prison Rape Elimination Commission, pp. 145–148.

Chapter 2

LGBTQI Youth under Custodial Supervision

Many corrections professionals are unaware that the youth they work with identify as lesbian, gay, bisexual, transgender, questioning, and intersex (LGBTQI), and many juvenile justice agencies do not have policies or provide training for their staff that pertains to LGBTQI youth. Research shows that LGBTQI youth represent as much as 15 percent of the total population of adjudicated youth.[75] Secure detention facilities can be particularly dangerous and hostile places for LGBTQI youth. Without policies and training, staff are unprepared to provide safe and professional care to this population. Transgender youth and youth with intersex conditions face additional challenges in detention because of housing and medical care.

Like other detained youth, transgender and intersex youth are generally placed in sex-segregated facilities according to external genitalia rather than gender identity.[76] When transgender girls or girls with intersex conditions are placed in boys' facilities, they are at very high risk for physical and sexual abuse by other youth and staff. In addition, some facilities do not provide transgender youth with medically necessary transition-related health care.[77] Having policies and procedures as well as staff training, however, can better equip agencies to make decisions that are balanced regarding both the safety of LGBTQI youth and the agency as a whole.

> "[B]ecause the state has no legitimate interest in punishment [of juveniles in custody], the conditions of juvenile confinement ... are subject to more exacting scrutiny than conditions imposed on convicted criminals."
>
> *Milonas v. Williams*, 691 F.2d 931, 942 n.10 (10th Cir. 1982).

I. The Law

LGBTQI youth in the juvenile justice system have established rights under the U.S. Constitution, state and federal statutes and regulations, and through court precedent. Understanding these rights can help juvenile justice agencies and staff develop appropriate policies and procedures for working with LGBTQI youth and provide for their safety and rehabilitation.

A. Constitutional Law

The U.S. Constitution extends critical rights to *all* detained youth. Juvenile justice agencies have an enhanced responsibility to ensure that youth in their custody are safe and free from unreasonably restrictive conditions of confinement.[78] Youth in juvenile justice settings are entitled to more protection than incarcerated adults, and courts use the 14th Amendment due process clause to analyze conditions of confinement claims.[79] Under the 14th Amendment, juvenile facilities are required to provide all youth in their custody with reasonable conditions of confinement and freedom from unreasonable bodily restraint, and to protect the right to be free from abuse and to receive adequate health care and fair and nondiscriminatory treatment.[80] Finally, confined youth maintain their right to freedom of expression and freedom of religion under the First Amendment. In 2006, an important piece of litigation exposed a pattern and practice of sexual and physical victimization of LGBTQI youth confined in the Hawaii Youth Correctional

Facility. In *R.G.* v. *Koller,* three LGBTQI youth filed a lawsuit in the U.S. District Court for the District of Hawaii, challenging the failure of facility staff to protect them from physical, emotional, and sexual abuse by other youth.[81] Ultimately, the court found that there was a pervasive climate of hostility toward, discrimination against, and harassment of youth based on their actual or perceived sexual orientation, sex, and/or transgender status. The court also found that acts of religious preaching by staff were content based and presented a discriminatory viewpoint that silenced the youth's speech regarding their lives as LGBTQI teenagers, their feelings, and their important relationships.[82]

1. Freedom from Abuse

Correctional administrators have a legal responsibility to ensure that staff intervene promptly to protect the safety of residents.[83] If staff are aware that a youth is being subjected to harassment or abuse, they must respond with appropriate actions designed to stop the harassment and/or abuse, especially if the targeted youth is known to be vulnerable because he/she is young, has a mental illness, is openly LGBTQI, or is perceived to be LGBTQI.[84] For that reason, agencies should have a sound classification system that prevents the placement of vulnerable youth (such as LGBTQI youth) with aggressive youth who may be abusive.[85]

2. Freedom from Isolation

All youth under supervision have a right to be free from unreasonably restrictive conditions of confinement, including isolation. Numerous courts have concluded that the use of administrative segregation or isolation in juvenile settings—even for short periods of time—is cruel, harmful, and unconstitutional.[86] Facilities and staff may violate this constitutional right if they place LGBTQI youth in isolation, either as punishment for expressing their identity or based on the myth that LGBTQI youth are sexually aggressive or a danger to other youth.[87] Placing all LGBTQI youth in segregation or isolation to protect them from abuse[88] and/or using isolation to separate LGBTQI youth from their abuser(s)[89] also violate youth's constitutional rights.

As one court has explained it, placing youth in isolation in response to an incident of abuse is akin to "attempting [ ] to remedy one harm with an indefensible and unconstitutional solution." Although an LGBTQI youth may be at risk of violence in a juvenile facility, the Constitution requires a more effective and less stigmatizing response than isolation.[90]

Staff should not treat LGBTQI youth as sex offenders, house them with sex offenders, or send them to sex offender treatment programs because of their gender identity or sexual orientation.[91] Facilities may violate youth's constitutional rights by labeling or treating LGBTQI youth as sex offenders or housing them with sex offenders without adequate due process protections such as a hearing, an evaluation by a qualified mental health professional, and an opportunity to appeal the designation and/or placement.

In *Smith* v. *Wade,* the court found that the failure of facility authorities to separate aggressive youth from potential victims could demonstrate callous or reckless indifference, making them liable for the injury of the endangered youth.

Smith v. *Wade,* 461 U.S. 30 (1983).

In *R.G.* v. *Koller,* the court found that the Hawaii Youth Correctional Facility:

· Failed to protect the plaintiffs from physical, sexual, and psychological abuse.

· Used isolation as a means to protect LGBT youth from abuse.

· Failed to provide the policies and training necessary to protect LGBT youth.

· Did not have adequate staffing and supervision or a functioning grievance system.

· Failed to use a classification system that protects vulnerable youth.

R.G. v. *Koller,* 415 F. Supp. 2d 1129 (D. Hawaii 2006).

3. The Right to Adequate Medical Care

All detained youth have a right to receive adequate physical and mental health care,[92] including health care that may be unique to that youth.[93] Agencies should provide appropriate medical and mental health care to transgender youth who are diagnosed with gender dysphoria, including access to medical providers with specific experience in evaluating and treating gender dysphoria in adolescents. In the adult context, courts have found that "transsexualism" constitutes a "serious medical need"; therefore, deliberately denying access to transgender-related health care amounts to cruel and unusual punishment.[94] Given the lower legal standard that applies to youth, agencies must provide appropriate care to address youth's medical and mental health needs with regard to gender identity.

4. Freedom of Speech and Expression

All youth have a constitutional right to freedom of speech and freedom of expression, which includes the right to be open about one's sexual orientation[95] and the right to express one's gender through clothing and grooming practices.[96] Because youth in custodial settings are still meeting adolescent development markers, it may be harmful to youth's development to require them to hide their sexual orientation or gender identity. Policies that do not allow youth, especially gender-nonconforming youth, to express their gender through clothing and accessories can be counterproductive to normal adolescent development.[97] In particular, self-expression through clothes and grooming is a normal part of adolescent development, and juvenile justice agencies should consider this when developing policies that are rigid regarding clothing and grooming practices. Safety of all youth is paramount, but safety is not necessarily inconsistent with allowing youth to express themselves through clothing and grooming when appropriate.

5. The Right to Religious Freedom

The First Amendment guarantees youth in juvenile facilities the right to religious freedom and the right to be free from religious indoctrination.[98] Juvenile justice agencies that require LGBTQI youth to hide their identities or participate in religious activities that they object to, that condemn homosexuality and gender differences, or that try to convert LGBTQI youth may violate youth's First Amendment rights. Additionally, staff who intimidate or coerce LGBTQI youth into adopting a particular religious practice or belief also violate the First Amendment.[99]

6. Reparative Therapies

Churches and other religious groups have routinely engaged in the practice of conversion therapy in an attempt to change an individual's sexual attraction from homosexual to heterosexual.[100] In 2012, one of the largest and most prominent of these conversion groups, Exodus International, announced that it would no longer practice or promote conversion therapy.[101] To explain the group's disassociation from conversion therapy, Alan Chambers (president of Exodus International) stated that "'99.9 percent' of the people he had met through Exodus International either had not changed their sexual attraction or still struggled with temptation."[102]

To further acknowledge the ineffectiveness of conversion therapy, California became the first state to ban sexual orientation change efforts for minors. The California law states that "[u]nder no circumstances shall a mental health provider engage in sexual orientation change efforts with a patient under 18 years of age."[103] The law further states that

> **Members shall:**
>
> "respect and protect the civil and legal rights of all probation youth."
>
> "refrain from discriminating against any individual because of race, gender, creed, national origin, religious affiliation, age, disability, or any other type of prohibited discrimination."
>
> "respect, promote, and contribute to a workplace that is safe, healthy, and free of harassment in any form."
>
> American Correctional Association, Code of Ethics, 1994, *http://www.aca.org/pastpresentfuture/ethics.asp.*

any effort to change sexual orientation "by a mental health provider shall be considered unprofessional conduct and shall subject a mental health provider to discipline by the licensing entity for that mental health provider."[104] Mental health professionals challenged this law on constitutional grounds in two separate cases in the U.S. District Court for the Eastern District of California; the presiding judges reached opposite conclusions.[105] The ninth circuit is expected to hear the merits of the constitutional argument in 2013.

II. National Prison Rape Elimination Act Standards

The Prison Rape Elimination Act (PREA) requires juvenile justice agencies to screen youth for risk of sexual victimization and abuse. At a minimum, the intake screening must ascertain any gender-nonconforming appearance and consider whether the resident is or is perceived to be LGBTQI,[106] the youth's perception of his or her own vulnerability,[107] and any additional information that "may indicate heightened needs for supervision, additional safety precautions, or separation from certain other residents."[108] The facility shall not place LGBTQI youth "in particular housing, bed, or other assignments solely on the basis of such identification or status" nor consider LGBTQI status "as an indicator of likelihood of being sexually abusive."[109]

In deciding whether to assign a transgender or intersex youth to a particular facility for male or female residents, and in making other housing and programming assignments, the agency should consider (on a case-by-case basis) whether a placement would ensure the youth's health and safety and whether the placement would present management or security problems. The transgender or intersex youth's "own view with respect to his or her own safety shall be given serious consideration."[110] Lastly, transgender and intersex youth must be able to shower separately from other residents.[111] Agencies must reassess these placement and programming assignments for transgender and intersex youth at least twice per year.[112] If a youth is isolated due to the risk of sexual victimization or abuse, the facility must document the basis for its concern for the youth's safety and provide the reason(s) why "no alternative means of separation can be arranged."[113] Every 30 days, the facility must review each isolated youth's situation to determine whether the need for continued separation from the general population persists.[114]

A juvenile agency is not permitted to "search or physically examine a transgender or intersex resident for the sole purpose of determining the resident's genital status." A resident's genital status can only be ascertained "during conversations with the resident, by reviewing medical records, or, if necessary, by learning that information as part of a broader medical examination conducted in private by a medical practitioner."[115] Furthermore, the agency must train staff to conduct cross-gender searches and searches of transgender and intersex residents in a "professional and respectful manner, and in the least intrusive manner possible, consistent with security needs."[116]

Finally, the PREA standards provide guidance for agencies on staff training, investigations, and data collection with regard to LGBTQI residents. Each agency must train employees who may have contact with youth to communicate effectively and professionally with those who identify as LGBTQI.[117] Agencies are permitted to prohibit all sexual activity but may not "deem such activity to constitute sexual abuse if it determines that the activity is not coerced."[118] When conducting incident reviews of abusive sexual acts, the agency must "[c]onsider whether the incident or allegation was motivated by ... gender identity; lesbian, gay, bisexual, transgender, or intersex identification, status, or perceived status ... or was motivated or otherwise caused by other group dynamics at the facility."[119]

III. Other Governing Principles: State Human Rights Law and Professional Codes of Ethics

In addition to the protections provided by the U.S. Constitution, some states also have statutes or regulations that prohibit discrimination based on sexual orientation and gender identity or expression in juvenile justice facilities. State laws that provide protection for LGBTQI youth in custody include (1) nondiscrimination laws specific to juvenile facilities or state-funded programs, (2) nondiscrimination laws for people in institutional settings, (3) public accommodation laws, and (4) housing laws.[120]

Codes of ethics of the American Correctional Association and the National Juvenile Detention Association (NJDA) outline the responsibilities that juvenile justice professionals owe to all youth in their care, including LGBTQI youth.[121] The NJDA Code of Ethics requires juvenile detention workers to (1) not tolerate "discrimination ... or any form of child abuse," (2) refuse to remain silent when youth's rights are violated and "speak on behalf of the affected youths," and (3) respond in a timely and appropriate manner to all harassment and abuse to alleviate conditions that could cause harm.[122]

IV. Elements of Legally Sound and Effective Policy and Practice

All LGBTQI policies should be based on the following guiding principles:[123]

- Respectful interactions between youth and between staff and youth.
- Do no harm.
- Safety of youth who are vulnerable.
- Targeted to your legal obligations and what you are required to do by law.

In addition, all LGBTQI policies should include the following elements:

- Statement of purpose.
- Enumeration of included groups.
- Prohibitions.
- Requirements.
- Scope of applicability.
- Definitions.
- Responsibilities.
- Enforcement and sanctions (for both staff and youth).
- Training and dissemination methods.

The following areas should be addressed when developing, revising, and/or implementing facility policies to ensure the safety of LGBTQI youth in custodial settings:

- Nondiscrimination.
- Intake.

- Risk assessment.
- Classification.
- Communication.
- Medical care.
- Mental health care.
- Privacy.
- Safety.

Each of these areas is discussed in greater detail below. Each section includes a discussion of the purpose for adopting a specific policy and a list of questions to consider when drafting or revising policies and procedures. Policies should fill the gap between what is required under the law and what should be done as good correctional practice. Appendix D includes examples of agency policies that address some of these issues.

A. Nondiscrimination Policies

Juvenile justice agencies should develop, adopt, and enforce policies that include zero tolerance for discrimination and mistreatment of youth and staff based on actual or perceived sexual orientation and gender identity or expression. These policies should specifically prohibit harassment and abuse of youth and staff by staff or other youth.

Following are questions to ask regarding an agency's nondiscrimination policy:

NONDISCRIMINATION POLICY CHECKLIST	YES	NO
Does the agency have a nondiscrimination policy for youth, employees, and/or volunteers?		
Does the agency policy require that all individuals who enter the agency are treated with fairness, dignity, and respect regardless of real or perceived sexual orientation?		
Does the agency policy explicitly list sexual orientation and gender identity or expression as prohibited bases for discrimination?		
Does the agency policy prohibit attempts by staff to ridicule or change a youth's sexual orientation or gender identity?		
Does the agency policy define staff duty to provide safe and healthy environments in which all individuals are treated with respect and dignity?		
Does the agency policy define staff responsibility for protecting the civil rights of LGBTQI youth while in custody, and for ensuring their physical and emotional well-being and safety in juvenile facilities?		
Does the agency policy define the elements of incident reporting to include complaints of harassment, discrimination, and abuse?		
Does the agency policy provide training and resources regarding the societal, familial, and developmental challenges confronting LGBTQI youth?		
Does the agency policy address the collection and analysis of data regarding the needs of LGBTQI youth in its custody?		

If the answer to most of these questions is "yes," it is likely that the agency is close to being in line with federal and state laws and regulations as well as constitutional provisions for LGBTQI youth. If the answer to most of these questions is "no," it may indicate that the agency has some work to do in this area, and a policy revision based on the legal rights outlined above and in the PREA standards is in order. Sample nondiscrimination policies are available at *http://www.wcl.american.edu/endsilence/juvenile_policies.cfm.*

B. Intake, Risk Assessment, and Classification

1. Intake and Risk Assessment

Identifying safety concerns for LGBTQI youth is a priority in determining risk. Agencies should develop and implement intake processes to identify LGBTQI youth and those perceived to be LGBTQI who are vulnerable to physical and sexual assault.

Following are questions to ask regarding an agency's intake and risk assessment policy and practice:

INTAKE AND RISK ASSESSMENT POLICY CHECKLIST	YES	NO
During intake and initial classification, does the agency ascertain information about the youth's sexual orientation and/or gender identity?		
During the course of the youth's confinement, does the agency periodically update information regarding the youth's sexual orientation and gender identity?		
Do the agency employees who conduct initial screening and classification receive training regarding sensitivity in conducting interviews with LGBTQI youth?		
Does the agency policy require that a youth's sexual orientation and/or gender identity be verified by multiple sources prior to classification?		
Are medical health practitioners the only staff permitted to physically examine youth to gather information about gender identity?*		
Does the agency policy have a process to document and accommodate the concerns of LGBTQI youth in terms of safety, name, pronoun, showering, and searches?		
Do the agency medical and mental health staff use screening tools that are developed specifically for LGBTQI youth?		
Does the agency provide youth orientation that discusses diversity and describes the harms that result from name-calling, bullying, and harassment?		

* Although PREA permits medical examiners to physically examine youth to ascertain information about their gender identity, pediatric physicians question whether subjecting a youth to such an examination is medically safe practice. See *PREA Standards and Policy Development Guidelines for Lesbian, Gay, Bisexual and Transgender Youth in Custody,* The Project on Addressing Prison Rape, November 13, 2012, *http://www.wcl.american.edu/endsilence/webinars.cfm.*

If the answer to most of these questions is "no," the agency will need to rewrite its policy to be more in line with the PREA standards that address risk assessment and screening. Risk assessment and screening are crucial to the safety of LGBTQI youth, especially when those are the tools and policies in place to inform housing options for youth in custody. All screening tools should include vulnerability assessments, the types of housing decisions that can be made by staff, and a stipulation as to when an assessment requires moving a decision up the chain of command. Housing and classification are key to ensuring the safety of youth.

2. Classification

Juvenile facilities must have sound classification systems that separate vulnerable youth from aggressive youth. In classifying youth, facilities must not infringe on the youth's right to be free from unreasonably restrictive conditions (such as isolation) and practices that amount to punishment without due process (such as automatic placement based on gender identity). Facilities should use all information obtained during intake to make all housing, bed, program, education, and work assignments for youth, with the goal of keeping all youth physically and emotionally safe.

Following are questions to ask regarding an agency's classification policy:

CLASSIFICATION POLICY CHECKLIST	YES	NO
Is the agency classification policy based on individualized needs that balance the youth's physical and emotional well-being with the safety of all other youth?		
Is the agency classification process objective and free of individual biases?		
Is the agency classification process defined in written policies and procedures?		
Does the agency prohibit blanket policies regarding the classification of LGBTQI youth or those perceived to be LGBTQI?		
Does the agency classification policy govern the placement of youth into sex offender programs/units based on articulated criteria, including orders of the court?		
Do the agency classification and housing protocols consider physical layout and privacy issues when determining the location for LGBTQI youth?		
Does the agency place vulnerable youth in the least restrictive environment necessary to ensure safety and provide the youth with equal access to facility services?		
Do the agency classification protocols address how youth in various classifications are housed if the facility is crowded?		
Do the agency classification and housing protocols consider privacy concerns when assigning housing for LGBTQI youth?		
Does the agency develop responses to abuse or harassment (or threat of abuse or harassment) of LGBTQI youth that do not rely on the isolation or segregation of these youth?		

As discussed above, confined youth have the right to be free from unreasonably restrictive conditions[124] and conditions or practices that amount to punishment.[125] Accordingly, instead of isolating LGBTQI youth, facility staff should implement more effective and fair safeguards such as "ensuring appropriate staff-to-resident ratios; modeling respectful behavior; providing close supervision of residents; promptly intervening to interrupt any disrespect, harassment or abuse directed at other youth; and keeping youth meaningfully engaged in constructive programming."[126] It is also essential (for safety and security as well as mental health care) that LGBTQI youth are not automatically treated as sex offenders, housed with sex offenders, or sent to sex offender treatment programs simply because of their gender identity or sexual orientation.[127]

Agencies should make housing determinations based on a number of factors, not based on LGBTQI status alone.[128] Additionally, agencies should not use youth's self-identification as LGBTQI "as an indicator of likelihood of being sexually abusive."[129]

C. Housing Specifications for Transgender and Intersex Youth

Determining gender-appropriate placements for transgender and intersex youth can be difficult. A handful of juvenile justice agencies[130] have clear written policies concerning housing placements for these youth. Agencies should make determinations for housing these youth on a case-by-case basis. Additionally, PREA standards advise agencies to make provisions for transgender and intersex youth to shower separately.[131]

Following are questions to ask regarding an agency's classification policy for transgender and intersex youth:

CLASSIFICATION FOR TRANSGENDER AND INTERSEX YOUTH POLICY CHECKLIST	YES	NO
Do the agency classification and housing policies include evaluation of a person's current genital status in making placement decisions?		
Does the agency make individualized housing determinations based on other factors in addition to a person's current genital status?		
Do the agency classification and housing policies include factors relating to the youth's emotional and physical well-being and that prioritize the youth's evaluation of his/her safety?		
Do the agency classification and housing policies include a review of youth's privacy concerns, available housing options, and recommendations from the youth's mental health providers regarding appropriate housing or classification?		
Does/can the agency provide access to private shower facilities, when necessary, or a single room for sleeping, while allowing youth to have full access to the facility's daily programming?		
Does/can the agency house transgender youth according to gender identity rather than birth sex?		
When it is necessary, can the agency place transgender youth safely according to birth sex and protect their physical and emotional well-being?		
Can the agency house transgender youth in a mixed-gender unit or program?		
Does the agency determine reclassification needs based on requests by youth or based on victimization?		

Individualized decisionmaking is key in making appropriate and ultimately safe housing decisions for LGBTQI youth. Currently, some agencies have policies that specifically call for individualized placement decisions for transgender and intersex individuals.

D. Respectful Communication

All policies for the safety and care of LGBTQI youth include components of respectful communication with and between all youth. Staff and volunteers should always be examples to youth, and should use respectful language and terminology that do not promote stereotypes about LGBTQI and questioning people or convey bias or hatred toward them. Additional elements of communication and/or harassment policies should include inclusive language and attention to names and pronouns. If professionals are unsure of a youth's gender identity, they should simply ask the youth about it and about the pronoun and name the youth uses.

Following are questions to ask regarding an agency's respectful communication policy for youth:

RESPECTFUL COMMUNICATION WITH YOUTH POLICY CHECKLIST	YES	NO
Does the agency have a zero-tolerance policy for sexual harassment, including harassment by staff and youth-on-youth harassment?		
Does the agency policy include direction to staff on how to address LGBTQI youth using respectful and appropriate language?		
If the agency policy permits youth to wear clothing other than issued clothing, does the agency policy permit youth to express themselves through clothing or grooming (within the bounds of safety for all youth)?		
Does the agency policy address confidentiality of information, including staff disclosure relating to the privacy and confidentiality of LGBTQI youth?		
Does the agency policy adhere to all confidentiality and privacy protections afforded LGBTQI youth under applicable state law?		
Does the agency policy allow for sharing of information necessary to achieve a particular purpose, such as identifying an appropriate placement in another facility?		
Does the agency policy provide for eligible LGBTQI youth to access programming and services within facilities?		

Juvenile agencies can allow youth to express their gender identity by giving them choices about clothing (including undergarments), hairstyle, and personal grooming. Agencies should give males and females the ability to choose between available clothing and grooming items (e.g., boxers or briefs, shaving supplies, and hair products). Allowing transgender youth to express their gender identity through choice of clothing (if such a choice is available), name, hairstyle, and other means of expression can contribute to positive mental health.

Confidentiality is a key component of honest communication with LGBTQI youth. Some youth will freely reveal this information to anyone who asks; others might not feel as comfortable discussing their identity or they might want to keep it from friends or parents. Staff should respect this and hold in confidence youth's sexual orientation or gender identity unless youth have given them permission to discuss it. This principle applies even in situations where staff feel that revealing information about a youth's sexual orientation or gender identity is in the youth's best interests. Doing so could immediately compromise a youth's safety in the facility and later compromise his/her safety at home or at school. Within the agency, any disclosure of information related to a youth's LGBTQI status should be limited to information necessary to achieve a specific beneficial purpose for that youth; in these circumstances, the information should only be disclosed to individuals who have a need to know.

E. Medical and Mental Health Care

At a minimum, policies on medical and mental health should provide all youth with access to quality medical care. LGBTQI youth should have opportunities to receive counseling as well as medical health care that meets their unique needs. Agencies should not attempt to change youth's sexual orientation or gender identity, punish youth for expressing their sexual orientation or gender identity, or require youth to undergo sex offender counseling based solely on the youth's sexual orientation or gender identity.

Following are questions to ask regarding an agency's medical and mental health care policy for LGBTQI youth:

MEDICAL AND MENTAL HEALTH CARE POLICY CHECKLIST	YES	NO
Do the agency medical and mental health protocols include opportunities for LGBTQI youth to access services that address self-acceptance and validation, concerns about disclosure of sexual orientation or gender identity, family relationships, healthy intimate relationships, and sexual decisionmaking?		
Does the agency policy promote the hiring of medical and mental health professionals who have expertise and/or experience in working with LGBTQI youth?		
In assessing a youth's medical and/or mental health status, does the agency policy direct medical staff to include an assessment of the youth's safety?		
Do the agency medical and mental health protocols direct those conducting medical screening to inquire about the inmate's sexual activity, sexual orientation, and gender identity, both before and during confinement?		
Do the agency medical protocols provide for gynecological and obstetrical care?		
Do the agency medical protocols provide for HIV and STD testing, care, and confidentiality?		
Do the agency medical and mental health protocols provide for counseling for sexual trauma that occurred either before or during confinement?		
Do the agency medical and mental health protocols provide for mental health evaluations that include assessment of an array of mental health diagnoses, including gender dysphoria?		
Do the agency medical protocols address medical care for transgender youth, including evaluation of their care prior to incarceration?		

At a minimum, agencies should ensure that youth have access to medical personnel who are knowledgeable about the particular health needs of LGBTQI youth—especially transgender youth and youth with intersex conditions. If a transgender youth or a youth with intersex conditions requests an evaluation or treatment, facility staff should provide the youth with access to appropriate professionals and should provide all medically necessary treatment recommended. If the facility cannot provide treatment onsite, then the youth should be transported to the provider. If a transgender youth or a youth with an intersex condition has been receiving medical and/or mental health services (such as hormone treatments) prior to arriving at the facility, the facility should consult with the youth's medical providers and continue to provide medically necessary treatment.

F. Privacy and Safety

Facilities should provide access to private bathrooms and showers (when necessary) or a single room for sleeping. Privacy accommodations should not prevent LGBTQI youth from full integration into the facilities' daily programming. In general, policies that are integral to addressing the safety and privacy issues and concerns of LGBTQI youth include:

- Cross-gender supervision.

- Use of facilities—bathrooms, showers, etc.

- Search procedures.

- Undressing.

Following are questions to ask regarding an agency's privacy and safety policy for youth:

PRIVACY AND SAFETY POLICY CHECKLIST	YES	NO
Does the agency practice cross-gender supervision of youth? If the answer is "yes" or "no," explain what that means.		
Does the agency policy address levels of staffing and supervision?		
Does the agency policy address the safety and privacy needs of LGBTQI youth in regard to toileting, showering, and sleeping?		
Do transgender or intersex youth have the option of choosing to be strip-searched by staff members of either gender?		
Does the agency policy address search procedures and privacy needs of LGBTQI youth?		
Does the agency policy require that youth grievances be tracked, and does the agency collect and analyze information on grievances related to searches?		

To develop sound policy in these areas, facility administrators should focus on ways in which the facility can protect the privacy, dignity, and safety of LGBTQI youth. Policies should avoid subjecting transgender youth to unnecessary risks of physical and emotional harm. Facilities should act on a case-by-case basis and encourage staff members to work with transgender youth to determine the best solution for accessing the bathroom, showering, changing clothing, searches, and drug testing that protects their privacy, dignity, and safety.

G. Sexual Abuse of LGBTQI Youth

Not all sexual behaviors between youth in facilities can be categorized as sexual abuse. Many times, youth voluntarily engage in sexual activities. Exploring sexuality and sexual identity is a key component of adolescent development. Therefore, agencies should have policies that require staff to determine whether an incident of sexual behavior between youth is sexual abuse or noncoercive voluntary sexual activity. Although voluntary sexual activity between youth may violate agency policies, it may not violate state criminal laws and is not prohibited by the PREA standards. However, it is important to recognize there is a continuum regarding youth's engagement in sexual behavior while in custody. Sexual behavior between youth can be nonabusive or abusive; however, it can also be strategic (i.e., sex for trade) or coerced (i.e., sex for protection). On any given day, encounters can move along the continuum—consensual one day and coercive the next. Therefore, agencies must recognize these elements of sexual behavior in custody and have policies that pay special attention to the fact that LGBTQI youth have increased vulnerability to abuse.

Following are questions to ask regarding an agency's sexual abuse policy for youth:

SEXUAL ABUSE POLICY CHECKLIST	YES	NO
Does the agency policy prohibit the sexual abuse of youth in custody?		
Does the agency policy stipulate that staff must receive training regarding the sexuality and sexual behaviors of youth?		
Does the agency policy require the investigation of all reports of violations of policy regarding sexual abuse?		
Does the agency have multiple methods for youth to report sexual abuse, including avenues for third-party, independent reporting?		
Does the agency policy address the treatment and management of youth who report allegations of sexual abuse?		
Does the agency policy define acceptable sexual behavior for youth and sanctions for violations?		
Does the agency policy define the roles and responsibilities of the investigative process into allegations of sexual abuse?		
Does the agency policy (or the investigative entity's policy) require referral of allegations of potential criminal activity for review by the prosecutor?		
Does the agency policy require a review of reports and investigations of sexual abuse?		
Does the agency policy establish a sexual assault response team?		
Do the agency protocols provide for ongoing medical and mental health care for youth who have been sexually victimized while in custody?		
Does the agency policy recognize particularly vulnerable populations, such as LGBTQI youth, and identify their need for treatment?		

Chapter 3

LGBTI Adults under Custodial Supervision

Similar to staff in juvenile facilities, many adult correctional professionals are ill-prepared to work with inmates who identify as lesbian, gay, bisexual, transgender, and intersex (LGBTI), and most agencies do not have policies or provide training for staff related to working with LGBTI inmates. Without essential policies and training, staff are unprepared to provide safe and professional care to this population, especially given the challenges that LGBTI inmates present in securing safe housing and medical and mental health care.

I. The Law

Like all other incarcerated individuals, those who identify as LGBTI and are held in adult facilities have rights under the U.S. Constitution and under state and federal statutes and regulations. Understanding how these rights apply to LGBTI people can help criminal justice professionals develop policies and procedures that provide for the safety of LGBTI people and can also help correctional agencies meet their legal obligations.

A. Constitutional Law

The Eighth Amendment to the U.S. Constitution gives citizens the right to be free from cruel and unusual punishment, which includes safety and adequate medical care in correctional settings.[132] Additionally, the U.S. Constitution provides the right to receive nondiscriminatory treatment under the 5th and 14th Amendments, and limited rights to privacy under the due process clause. Individuals also retain limited rights to freedom of religion, expression, and association, even while incarcerated.

> Spreading rumors that a person is gay has been held to state a claim of deliberate indifference under the Eighth Amendment because "in the prison context … one can think of few acts that could be more likely to lead to physical injury than spreading rumors of homosexuality."
>
> *Thomas v. District of Columbia*, 887 F. Supp. 1, 4 (D.D.C. 1995); *see also Montero v. Crusie*, 153 F. Supp. 2d 368, 378 (S.D. N.Y. 2001).

1. Eighth Amendment Protections from Physical and Sexual Abuse

Corrections agencies have a responsibility to protect inmates from abuse at the hands of other inmates and staff, including volunteers and contractors. Agency officials can be held liable under the Eighth Amendment's cruel and unusual punishment clause if they are deliberately indifferent and fail to protect inmates. In 1994, the U.S. Supreme Court held that prison officials cannot be deliberately indifferent to the sexual abuse of a transgender inmate who was repeatedly raped and beaten by other inmates.[133] The Court explained that officials are liable for abuse of inmates when "the official knows of and disregards an excessive risk to inmate health or safety."[134] An excessive risk exists when an inmate belongs to "an identifiable group of people who are frequently singled out for violent attack by other inmates."[135] Since that finding, numerous courts have found that an inmate's LGBTI status or gender nonconformity alone may be sufficient to put agency officials on notice of that individual's vulnerability and need for protection.[136] Failure to take adequate protective measures in the face of this vulnerability can and generally does constitute deliberate indifference.[137] In 2004, the sixth circuit noted that "placing a transgender woman in protective custody with inmates who have assaulted other inmates resulted in a substantial risk to her safety and could amount to deliberate indifference."[138]

2. Use of Administrative Segregation for Protection

Although it is permissible to place vulnerable inmates in administrative segregation in some circumstances, agency officials will not be able to rely on this measure as long-term protection for LGBTI inmates. Whether it violates the U.S. Constitution to place vulnerable inmates in administrative segregation depends on the purpose of segregation, the availability of other alternatives to provide protection, the harshness or restrictiveness of the conditions in segregation, the duration of segregation, and whether the appropriateness of segregation for a particular inmate is regularly reviewed.[139] Agency officials may, however, segregate LGBTI inmates as a temporary measure when there are specific circumstances, such as upon admission (while determining an appropriate long-term placement) or immediately following an assault and during a pending investigation.[140]

3. Medical Care for LGBTI Inmates

On multiple occasions, the U.S. Supreme Court found that deliberate indifference to a person's serious medical needs violates the Eighth Amendment.[141] An inmate is denied medical care when officials either refuse to provide medical care or are so incompetent that, for all intents and purposes, they fail to provide care. However, this does not suggest that an LGBTI inmate is entitled to the care of his/her choosing. Courts have recognized that the denial of "desired accommodations and medical treatment" does not violate inmates' rights under the 8th or 14th Amendment.[142] One example is the refusal to provide hormone therapy for transgender inmates. On the other hand, courts have recognized that transgender inmates with gender dysphoria have a serious medical condition, and that failure to treat inmates with this condition is a violation of the Eighth Amendment.[143] As with any other medical condition, courts will generally defer to the medical staff's treatment choices, but only if these choices result in treatments that are adequate and effective for treating a particular inmate's gender dysphoria needs.[144]

Factors such as the length of imprisonment and custody are also relevant. The treatment required in a short-term jail or lockup will differ from that required in a prison. Medical care for inmates with gender dysphoria should be based on an individualized medical evaluation that determines what care is medically necessary for particular inmates. To meet this standard, correctional administrators should avoid policies that only permit proscribed treatments (such as psychotherapy or antidepressants) to treat gender dysphoria. Policies that specifically prohibit hormone therapy for inmates with gender dysphoria, especially those who were not receiving hormones at the time of incarceration, are not in accordance with the standards of care for gender dysphoria.[145] A federal district court found that a prison may not adopt a "rigid, freeze-frame policy," where inmates with gender dysphoria have access only to the specific treatments they received prior to incarceration.[146]

Some courts have found that the harmful physiological and psychological effects stemming from the discontinuation of hormone therapy amount to deliberate indifference. Conversely, the U.S. District Court for the Western District of Texas has ruled that an inmate with gender identity disorder (GID) was not entitled to receive hormone therapy, stating that the inmate's "disagreement with the course of treatment pursued by prison medical staff does not constitute a viable claim for deliberate indifference to serious medical needs under the Eighth Amendment."[147]

Courts have found that correctional policies that restrict certain treatments for all inmates with gender dysphoria "irrespective of an inmate's serious medical need or the [prison medical professional's] clinical judgment" are impermissible.[148] As one court explained, "there is no exception to [the Eighth Amendment] for serious medical needs that are first diagnosed in prison."[149] Additionally, if the treatment prescribed after a medical evaluation is not consistent with the patient's diagnosis, or when the evaluation is conducted by someone without appropriate knowledge of gender dysphoria, inmates can challenge the adequacy of the medical evaluation and treatment.[150]

Court findings indicate that agencies cannot deny treatment for inmates with gender dysphoria based on a generalized or unsubstantiated security concern, or based on concerns that relate to the inmate's transgender status or gender expression. When treatment would present a security risk, corrections officials must balance these concerns against the medical necessity of the treatment.[151] Finally, medical treatment cannot be denied to a person with gender dysphoria simply because it is expensive or because it might be unpopular or controversial to prescribe such treatment.[152]

4. Gender Presentation and Expression

Denying inmates with gender dysphoria the ability to fully adopt the gender role and presentation consistent with their gender identities can constitute a denial of necessary medical care and a violation of the Eighth Amendment.[153]

Another treatment frequently required for individuals with gender dysphoria is "Real Life Experience."[154] This treatment consists of expressing the gender that is consistent with one's gender identity in all aspects of everyday life. Some courts have recognized that Real Life Experience is a legitimate and often essential form of treatment for gender dysphoria in the correctional context, and may at times be medically necessary and constitutionally required.[155] In contrast, the U.S. District Court of Kansas has held that a biologically male inmate did not have a constitutional right to receive cosmetics and female clothing.[156]

In *Kosilek* v. *Maloney, the* U.S. District Court for the District of Massachusetts determined that Real Life Experience was possible in prison, based on the testimony of medical experts that prison is an inmate's "real life."[157] In 2012, the same court found that prison officials had been deliberately indifferent to Kosilek's serious medical need, and ordered the Massachusetts Department of Corrections to provide sex reassignment surgery.[158] The U.S. District Court for the Western District of Virginia reached an opposite conclusion, ruling on summary judgment that Ophelia De'Lonta, a male-to-female transgender inmate, was not entitled to surgical intervention to treat her severe GID.[159] The fourth circuit, however, reversed and remanded the lower court's ruling, finding that De'Lonta is entitled to a hearing on the merits of her case.[160]

Agency officials can be held liable for deliberate indifference to a person's serious medical need by denying, delaying, or intentionally interfering with his or her medical treatment.

See, e.g., *Estelle* v. *Gamble*, 429 U.S. 97 (1976).

When determining whether a particular treatment for gender dysphoria is adequate, courts have looked at:

- Whether it was provided for the purpose of treating gender dysphoria.
- Whether it is a reasonable and effective method for treating gender dysphoria.
- Whether it is tailored to meet the person's particular medical needs.

See, e.g., *Soneeya* v. *Spencer*, 851 F. Supp. 2d 228 (D. Mass. 2012).

The U.S. District Court for the Eastern District of Wisconsin held that "a reasonable jury could find that the defendants were deliberately indifferent to Konitzer's serious medical need when they failed to provide [her] with the second step of treatment from the standards of care, the real-life experience..."

Konitzer v. *Frank*, 711 F. Supp. 2d 874, 908 (E.D. Wis. 2010).

5. Searches and Discrimination

If correctional officers target LGBTI people for unnecessarily public strip searches, it can violate the rights of inmates to be free from cruel and unusual punishment. Some courts have found that inmates have a clearly established right "not to be subjected to a humiliating strip search in full view of several (or perhaps many) others unless the procedure is *reasonably* related to a *legitimate* penological interest."[161] In *Meriwether* v. *Faulkner*, the seventh circuit held that a male-to-female transgender inmate stated a valid Eighth Amendment claim, where a correctional officer repeatedly demanded that the inmate strip in front of inmates and other officers for the sole purpose of viewing her body.[162] The court found this was sufficient to state an Eighth Amendment claim because the searches were "maliciously motivated" and not related to security matters.[163]

Courts have found that discrimination in providing services and privileges based on sexual orientation is a violation of constitutionally held rights. For example, correctional agencies may not prohibit visits by same-sex partners or include restrictions on affection between individuals of the same sex during visits where these same restrictions do not apply to heterosexual couples.

Courts have also ordered agencies to stop enforcing policies that prohibit visitation by same-sex partners of inmates. Denying such visits for the purposes of security is not constitutional.[164] Similarly, the ninth circuit denied a prison's motion to dismiss in a challenge to a state's complete ban on same-sex hugging and kissing among inmates and visitors who were not blood related, rejecting the contention that the policy bore a "common-sense" relation to prison security.[165] Some state departments of corrections, including the California Department of Corrections and Rehabilitation, have opted to extend conjugal visits to registered domestic partners.[166] Some agencies, however, retain policies that limit conjugal visits to legally married inmates.[167]

Courts have also prohibited other forms of discrimination. Agencies cannot deny LGBTI people permission to attend religious services based on their sexual orientation,[168] nor can they fire or refuse to hire eligible inmates based solely on their sexual orientation.[169] Similarly, agencies cannot punish inmates because of their sexual orientation.[170]

6. Confidentiality and Disclosure of Medical Information

The constitutional right to privacy protects information concerning an inmate's sexual orientation, and correctional officers may not arbitrarily disclose this information. Courts have recognized a similarly strong privacy interest in disclosure of one's sexual orientation. Courts have clearly recognized that, even in the correctional context, a person has a "particularly compelling" constitutional privacy interest in certain highly personal information, including one's transgender identity or HIV status,[171] and disclosing such information without a legitimate penological reason is unconstitutional.[172]

Agencies that permit conjugal visits may not prohibit conjugal visits for legally married same-sex couples if other married couples are provided opportunities for conjugal visits.

Doe v. *Sparks*, 733 F. Supp. 227 (W.D. Pa. 1990).

Inmates in state prisons cannot be denied the right to marry someone of the same sex if marriage between same-sex individuals is legal in that state.

Turner v. *Safely*, 482 U.S. 78 (1987).

In *Powell* v. *Shriver*, a transgender woman housed in a women's prison was casually outed as transgender and HIV-positive by staff, which led to a pattern of harassment by staff and inmates and violated her right to privacy. In that case, the second circuit specifically acknowledged the "excruciatingly private and intimate nature of transsexualism" and that such disclosure may put inmates at heightened risk of abuse; the court found that the disclosure violated privacy rights of inmates.

Powell v. *Shriver*, 175 F.3d 107 (2d Cir. 1999).

7. Access to Materials with LGBTI Content

Providing access to LGBTI materials is often covered by the First Amendment. Courts find that agencies may restrict inmates' rights to receive publications that may cause a threat to the daily operation of a facility,[173] but restrictions are limited to publications that would potentially interfere with security, order, or discipline. Agencies may not prohibit material solely because it contains LGBTI content; they can, however, generally prohibit sexually explicit materials.[174] A publication that discusses LGBTI issues or sexual orientation is not necessarily sexually explicit; agencies must have other reasons for excluding such content.

II. National Prison Rape Elimination Act Standards

The final Prison Rape Elimination Act (PREA) standards include specific provisions for LGBTI and gender-nonconforming inmates according to facility type. Each correctional setting offers a varying degree of protection for LGBTI inmates. These are the minimum standards that must be met to be compliant with PREA. However, agencies can and should develop policies and practices that take into account the needs of LGBTI populations in their own facilities.

A. Adult Prisons and Jails

The final PREA standards require adult prisons and jails to conduct an intake screening within 72 hours of an inmate's arrival to assess that inmate's risk for sexual victimization or abuse. Specifically, the standards provide that "the intake screening shall consider, at a minimum ... whether the inmate is or is perceived to be gay, lesbian, bisexual, transgender, intersex, or gender nonconforming."[175] Furthermore, "an inmate's risk level shall be reassessed when warranted due to a referral, request, incident of sexual abuse, or receipt of additional information that bears on the inmate's risk of sexual victimization or abusiveness."[176] Inmates may not be disciplined for refusal to answer or failure to disclose complete information in response to questions regarding sexual orientation. Importantly, an agency may not place LGBTI inmates in "dedicated facilities, units, or wings solely on the basis of such identification or status"[177] unless that placement is consistent with an existing consent decree, legal settlement, or legal judgment.[178]

The standards also include protections specific to transgender and intersex inmates. First, the standards indicate that "in deciding whether to assign a transgender or intersex inmate to a facility for male or female inmates, and in making other housing and programming assignments, the agency shall consider on a case-by-case basis whether a placement would ensure the inmate's health and safety, and whether the placement would present management or security problems."[179] The "inmate's own view with respect to his or her own safety shall be given serious consideration."[180] Finally, transgender and intersex inmates must be able to shower separately from other inmates. Agencies must assess placement and programming assignments for transgender and intersex inmates at least twice per year.[181]

The standards also place limits on cross-gender viewing and searches. Agencies may not "search or physically examine a transgender or intersex inmate for the sole purpose of determining the inmate's genital status."[182] The facility is permitted to determine an inmate's genital status "during conversations with the inmate, by reviewing medical records, or, if necessary, by learning that information as part of a broader medical examination conducted in private by a medical practitioner."[183] The agency must train its staff in how to conduct cross-gender searches and searches of transgender and intersex people "in a professional and respectful manner, and in the least intrusive manner possible, consistent with security needs."[184]

The standards provide guidance for agency staff on employee training, investigation of sexual activity, and data collection responsibilities with regard to LGBTI inmates. All agencies are required to train employees on effective and professional communication with inmates, specifically LGBTI inmates.[185] Agencies are permitted to prohibit all sexual activity, but may not "deem such activity to constitute sexual abuse if it determines that the activity is not coerced."[186] Finally, in collecting data on sexual incidents, the facility "shall consider whether the incident or allegation was motivated by ... gender identity; lesbian, gay, bisexual, transgender, or intersex identification, status, or perceived status ... or was motivated or otherwise caused by other group dynamics at the facility."[187]

B. Lockups

Like all individuals confined in a lockup, LGBTI individuals in such a facility[188] receive more limited protections under the standards due to the temporary nature of these facilities. Agency staff must screen detainees for risk of sexual victimization or abuse. Staff must ask the detainee about his or her own perception of vulnerability[189] and shall consider the detainee's physical build and appearance to determine the risk of sexual victimization.[190]

A lockup facility is not permitted to "search or physically examine a transgender or intersex detainee for the sole purpose of determining the detainee's genital status."[191] The facility is permitted to determine an inmate's genital status "during conversations with the inmate, by reviewing medical records, or, if necessary, by learning that information as part of a broader medical examination conducted in private by a medical practitioner."[192] Furthermore, the lockup must train staff to conduct cross-gender, transgender, and intersex searches in a "professional and respectful manner, and in the least intrusive manner possible, consistent with security needs."[193]

Finally, in conducting sexual abuse incident reviews, the lockup must "[c]onsider whether the incident or allegation was motivated by ... gender identity; lesbian, gay, bisexual, transgender, or intersex identification, status, or perceived status ... or was motivated or otherwise caused by other group dynamics at the lockup."[194]

C. Community Corrections

The standards also require that LGBTI residents of community confinement facilities[195] be screened for risk of sexual victimization and abuse. The intake screening must consider whether the resident is or is perceived to be LGBTI or questioning.[196] Facilities must reassess a resident's risk level "when warranted due to a referral, request, incident of sexual abuse, or receipt of additional information that bears on the resident's risk of sexual victimization or abusiveness."[197]

When making housing and programming assignments for a transgender or intersex resident, "the agency shall consider on a case-by-case basis whether a placement would ensure the resident's health and safety, and whether the placement would present management or security problems."[198] The facility shall not place LGBTI residents "in dedicated facilities, units, or wings solely on the basis of such identification or status"[199] unless such placement is consistent with a consent decree, legal settlement, or legal judgment.[200] The facility must give serious consideration to the transgender or intersex resident's view about his/her safety.[201] Finally, transgender and intersex residents must be permitted to shower separately from other residents.[202]

The standards place limits on cross-gender viewing and searches. "The facility shall not search or physically examine a transgender or intersex resident for the sole purpose of determining the resident's genital status. The facility is permitted to determine an inmate's genital status "during conversations with the inmate, by reviewing medical records, or, if necessary, by learning that information as part of a broader medical examination conducted in private by a medical practitioner."[203] "The agency shall train security staff in how to conduct cross-gender pat-down searches, and searches of transgender and intersex residents, in a professional and respectful manner, and in the least intrusive manner possible, consistent with security needs."[204]

The standards also provide guidance for agency staff on training, investigation, and data collection with regard to LGBTI residents. The facility must train employees who may have contact with LGBTI residents to communicate effectively and professionally with them. Agencies are permitted to prohibit all sexual activity, but may not "deem such activity to constitute sexual abuse if it determines that the activity is not coerced."[205] When conducting incident reviews, the agency must "[c]onsider whether the incident or allegation was motivated by … gender identity; lesbian, gay, bisexual, transgender, or intersex identification, status, or perceived status … or was motivated or otherwise caused by other group dynamics at the facility."[206]

III. Elements of Legally Sound and Effective Policy and Practice

All policies should be based on the following guiding principles:[207]

■ Respectful interactions between inmates, residents, and staff; between inmates; and between residents.

■ Do no harm.

■ Safety of vulnerable inmates or residents.

■ Adoption of accepted correctional practice.

■ Accountability in operations.

■ Recognition of the agency's legal obligations.

In addition, all policies should include the following elements:

■ Statement of purpose.

■ Enumeration of included groups.

■ Prohibitions.

■ Requirements.

■ Scope of applicability.

■ Definitions.

■ Responsibilities.

■ Enforcement and sanctions (for both staff and inmates or residents).

■ Training and dissemination methods.

The following areas should be addressed when developing, revising, and/or implementing policies to ensure the safety of LGBTI inmates or residents in custodial settings:

■ Nondiscrimination.

■ Intake screening.

■ Risk assessment, classification, and housing.

■ Program participation.

- Respectful communication with LGBTI populations.
- Medical care.
- Mental health care.
- Privacy and safety.
- Transportation.
- Inmate orientation.
- Staff training.
- Volunteer and contractor training.

Each of these areas is discussed in greater detail below. Each section includes a discussion of the purpose for adopting a specific policy and a list of questions to consider when drafting or revising policies and procedures. Policies should fill the gap between what is required under the law and what should be done as good correctional practice. Appendix D includes examples of agency policies that address some of these issues.

A. Nondiscrimination Policies

Agencies should develop, adopt, and enforce policies that explicitly prohibit discrimination and mistreatment of inmates or residents on the basis of sex, age, race, national origin, disability, and actual or perceived sexual orientation and gender identity. These policies should specifically prohibit harassment and abuse of inmates or residents by staff or other inmates or residents based on gender identity or sexual orientation.

Following is a list of questions to ask regarding an agency's nondiscrimination policy:

NONDISCRIMINATION POLICY CHECKLIST	YES	NO
Does the agency have a nondiscrimination policy for employees, inmates, residents, and/or volunteers?		
Does the agency policy require all LGBTI inmates or residents to be treated with fairness, dignity, and respect?		
Does the agency policy prohibit attempts by staff to ridicule or change an inmate's or resident's sexual orientation or gender identity?		
Does the agency policy define staff duty to provide safe and healthy environments in which all individuals are treated with respect and dignity?		
Does the agency policy define staff responsibility for protecting the civil rights of LGBTI inmates or residents while in custody, and ensuring their physical and emotional well-being and safety in facilities?		
Does the agency policy define the elements of incident reporting to include complaints of harassment, discrimination, and abuse?		
Does the agency policy provide training and resources regarding the societal, familial, and developmental challenges confronting LGBTI inmates or residents?		
Does the agency policy address the collection and analysis of data regarding the needs of LGBTI inmates or residents in its custody?		
Does the agency use the collected data and analysis to make decisions?		
Does the agency policy require equal access to programming for LGBTI inmates or residents (not dependent on classification)?		
If the agency policy permits conjugal visits for heterosexual couples, does the policy also permit conjugal visits for same-sex couples?		

If the answer to most of these questions is "yes," it is likely that the agency is close to being in line with federal and state laws and regulations as well as constitutional provisions for LGBTI inmates or residents. If the answer to most of these questions is "no," it may indicate that the agency has some work to do in this area, and a policy revision based on the legal rights outlined above and in the PREA standards is in order.

B. Intake, Risk Assessment, and Classification

1. Intake and Risk Assessment

Identifying safety concerns for LGBTI inmates or residents is an important factor in determining risk. Agencies should develop and implement intake processes to identify and assess risk for LGBTI inmates or residents who are vulnerable to physical and sexual assault, taking the inmate's or resident's assessment of risk into consideration.

Following is a list of questions to ask regarding an agency's intake and risk assessment policy:

INTAKE AND RISK ASSESSMENT POLICY CHECKLIST	YES	NO
During intake and initial classification, does the agency ascertain information about the inmate's or resident's sexual orientation and/or gender identity?		
During the course of the inmate's or resident's incarceration, does the agency periodically update information regarding his/her sexual orientation and gender identity?		
Do the agency employees who conduct initial screening and classification receive training regarding sensitivity in conducting interviews with LGBTI inmates or residents?		
Does the agency policy require that an inmate's or resident's sexual orientation and/or gender identity be verified by multiple sources prior to classification?		
Are medical practitioners the only staff permitted to physically examine inmates or residents to gather information about gender identity?		
Does the agency policy have a process to document and accommodate the concerns of LGBTI inmates or residents in terms of safety, name, pronoun, shower preference, and searches?		
Do the agency medical and mental health staff use screening tools that are developed specifically for LGBTI inmates or residents?		
Does the agency policy require diversity training for employees that includes the impact of name-calling and harassment?		

If the answer to most of these questions is "no," the agency will need to revise its policy to be more in line with the PREA standards that address risk assessment and screening. Under the PREA standards, the intake screening must, at a minimum, consider whether the inmate or resident is or is perceived to be LGBTI or gender nonconforming.[208] Risk assessment and screening are crucial to the safety of LGBTI inmates and residents, especially when those are the tools and policies in place to inform housing options in custody. All screening tools should include vulnerability assessments, the types of housing decisions that can be made by staff, and a stipulation as to when an assessment requires moving a decision up the chain of command. Housing and classification determinations are key to ensuring safety and limiting agency liability.

2. Classification

Given the actual and potential harassment and abuse directed toward LGBTI inmates or residents, protecting their safety is unquestionably a legitimate concern.

Following is a list of questions to ask regarding an agency's classification policy:

CLASSIFICATION POLICY CHECKLIST	YES	NO
Is the agency classification policy based on individualized needs that balance the inmates' or residents' physical and emotional well-being and safety?		
Is the agency classification process objective and free of individual biases?		
Is the agency classification process defined in written policies and procedures?		
Does the agency prohibit blanket policies regarding the classification of LGBTI inmates or residents, or those perceived to be LGBTI?		
Does the agency classification policy govern the placement of inmates or residents into sex offender programs/units based on articulated criteria, including orders of the court?		
Do the agency classification and housing protocols consider physical layout and privacy issues when determining the location for an LGBTI inmate or resident?		
Does the agency place vulnerable inmates or residents in the least restrictive environment necessary to ensure safety and provide the inmates or residents with equal access to facility services?		
Do the agency classification protocols address how inmates or residents in various classifications are housed if the facility is crowded?		
Do the agency classification and housing protocols consider privacy concerns when assigning housing for LGBTI inmates or residents?		
Does the agency develop responses to abuse or harassment (or threat of abuse or harassment) of LGBTI inmates or residents that do not rely on the isolation or segregation of these inmates or residents?		

Some agencies respond to safety concerns by placing LGBTI inmates in administrative segregation or protective custody. However, instead of isolating LGBTI inmates, staff should consider other strategies as outlined in classification policies. The safety of inmates or residents can be achieved by ensuring appropriate staff-to-inmate ratios; modeling respectful behavior; providing close supervision of inmates or residents; promptly intervening to interrupt any disrespect, harassment, or abuse directed at other inmates or residents; and keeping inmates or residents meaningfully engaged in constructive programming.

Additionally, LGBTI inmates should only be classified and housed in sex offender units or programs consistent with the agency's policies and/or court orders. It is not appropriate to house LGBTI inmates in sex offender units solely because of their gender identity or sexual orientation.

3. Housing

Determining gender-appropriate housing for transgender and intersex inmates or residents may be a challenge. Some state and local correctional and law enforcement agencies have written policies concerning the housing of transgender and intersex inmates. These policies incorporate an individualized approach to housing, as recommended by the National Prison Rape Elimination Commission and the final PREA standards.

Following is a list of questions to ask regarding an agency's classification and housing policies for transgender and intersex inmates or residents:

CLASSIFICATION AND HOUSING POLICY CHECKLIST FOR TRANSGENDER AND INTERSEX INMATES OR RESIDENTS	YES	NO
Do the agency classification and housing policies include evaluation of a person's current genital status in making placement decisions?		
Do the agency classification and housing policies include factors relating to the inmates' or residents' emotional and physical well-being and that prioritize the inmates' or residents' evaluation of his/her safety?		
Do the agency classification and housing policies include a review of inmates' or residents' privacy concerns, available housing options, and recommendations from the inmates' or residents' mental health providers regarding appropriate housing or classification?		
Does/can the agency provide access to private shower facilities, when necessary, or a single room for sleeping, while allowing inmates or residents to have full access to the facility's daily programming?		
Does/can the agency place transgender inmates or residents according to their core gender identity rather than their birth sex?		
When it is necessary, can the agency place transgender inmates or residents safely according to birth sex to protect their physical and emotional well-being?		
Does the agency house transgender inmates or residents in a mixed-gender unit or program?		
Does the agency determine reclassification needs based on requests by inmates or residents or based on victimization?		

Individualized decisionmaking is key in making appropriate and ultimately safe housing decisions for LGBTI inmates and residents. Currently, some agencies have policies that specifically call for individualized placement decisions for transgender and intersex individuals.

C. Respectful Communication

Respectful communications between staff and inmates or residents should be the agency's objective, including how LGBTI inmates are addressed based on their gender preference.

Following is a list of questions to ask regarding an agency's respectful communication policy for inmates or residents:

RESPECTFUL COMMUNICATION WITH LGBTI INMATES OR RESIDENTS POLICY CHECKLIST	YES	NO
Does the agency have a zero-tolerance policy for sexual harassment, including harassment by staff and inmate-on-inmate or resident-on-resident harassment?		
Does the agency policy include direction to staff on how to address LGBTI inmates or residents using respectful and appropriate language?		
If the agency policy permits inmates or residents to wear clothing other than issued clothing, does the agency policy permit them to express themselves through clothing or grooming (within the bounds of safety for all inmates or residents)?		
Does the agency policy address confidentiality of information, including staff disclosure relating to the privacy and confidentiality of LGBTI inmates or residents?		
Does the agency policy adhere to all confidentiality and privacy protections afforded LGBTI inmates or residents under applicable state law?		
Does the agency policy allow for sharing of information necessary to achieve a particular purpose, such as identifying an appropriate placement in another facility?		
Does the agency policy provide for eligible LGBTI inmates or residents to access programming and services within facilities?		

LGBTI policies should consider addressing transgender inmates or residents by the name and pronoun that the inmate prefers. If an agency's policies allow inmates or residents to wear clothing other than that issued by the institution, consideration should be given to permitting inmates or residents to express their gender identity through clothing. Also, where appropriate, agencies may consider allowing inmates or residents to express their gender identity in matters of grooming.

Correctional staff should respect each inmate's or resident's privacy and should never disclose an inmate's or resident's sexual orientation or gender identity unless the inmate or resident has given them permission, or unless security or another important agency interest requires the disclosure.

D. Medical and Mental Health Care

At a minimum, policies on medical and mental health should provide all inmates and residents with access to appropriate medical and mental health care. LGBTI inmates or residents identified as needing mental health or medical care should receive the care they need. Agencies should work to ensure that medical personnel are knowledgeable about the health needs of LGBTI inmates or residents—especially transgender inmates or residents.

Following is a list of questions to ask regarding an agency's medical and mental health care policy for inmates or residents:

MEDICAL AND MENTAL HEALTH CARE POLICY CHECKLIST	YES	NO
Do the agency medical and mental health protocols include opportunities for LGBTI inmates or residents to access services that address self-acceptance and validation, concerns about disclosure of sexual orientation or gender identity, family relationships, healthy intimate relationships, and sexual decisionmaking?		
Does the agency policy promote the hiring of medical and mental health professionals who have expertise and/or experience in working with LGBTI inmates or residents?		
In assessing an inmate's or resident's medical and/or mental health status, does the agency policy direct medical staff to include an assessment of an inmate's or resident's safety?		
Do the agency medical and mental health protocols direct those conducting medical screening to inquire about the inmate's or resident's sexual activity, sexual orientation, and gender identity, both before and during incarceration?		
Do the agency medical protocols provide for gynecological and obstetrical care?		
Do the agency medical protocols provide for HIV and STD testing, care, and confidentiality?		
Do the agency medical and mental health protocols provide for counseling for sexual trauma that occurred either before or during incarceration?		
Do the agency medical and mental health protocols provide for mental health evaluations that include assessment of an array of mental health diagnoses, including gender dysphoria?		
Do the agency medical protocols address medical care for transgender inmates or residents, including evaluation of their care prior to incarceration?		

At a minimum, agencies should ensure that inmates or residents have access to medical personnel who are knowledgeable about the particular health needs of LGBTI people. LGBTI inmates or residents should have access to appropriate professionals who can provide all medically necessary treatment. If the facility cannot provide treatment onsite, then the inmates or residents should be transported to the provider. Any medical care an LGBTI inmate or resident receives prior to arriving at the facility, such as hormone treatments, should be continued upon arrival at the facility after consultation with the appropriate medical providers.

E. Privacy and Safety

Agency policy should address how transgender inmates or residents are housed by assessing their safety and privacy during toileting, showering, and sleeping. In general, policies that are integral to addressing the safety and privacy issues and concerns of LGBTI inmates or residents include:

■ Cross-gender supervision.

■ Use of facilities—bathrooms, showers, etc.

■ Search procedures.

■ Undressing.

Following is a list of questions to ask regarding an agency's privacy and safety policy for inmates:

PRIVACY AND SAFETY POLICY CHECKLIST	YES	NO
Does the agency practice cross-gender supervision of inmates or residents? If the answer is "yes" or "no," explain what that means.		
Does the agency policy address levels of staffing and supervision?		
Does the agency policy address the safety and privacy needs of LGBTI inmates or residents in regard to toileting, showering, and sleeping?		
Does the agency policy address how pat and strip searches of LGBTI inmates or residents are conducted?		
Does the agency policy address search procedures and privacy needs of LGBTI inmates or residents?		
Does the agency policy require that inmate or resident grievances be tracked, and does the agency collect and analyze information on grievances related to searches?		

The key to developing sound policy in these areas is to focus on ways in which the facility can protect the privacy, dignity, and safety of LGBTI inmates or residents during all facility procedures. Policies should avoid subjecting transgender inmates or residents to unnecessary risk of physical and emotional harm. This may need to be done on a case-by-case basis where staff members work with the transgender inmate or resident to determine the best solution for accessing the bathroom, showering, changing clothing, searches, and drug testing that protects their privacy, dignity, and safety.

F. Sexual Abuse of LGBTI Inmates or Residents

It is important for agencies to recognize all elements of sexual behavior in custody and to have policies that manage these behaviors. Policies should also pay special attention to the LGBTI inmates' or residents' increased vulnerability to abuse, reporting mechanisms, investigations, and discipline (if necessary).

Following is a list of questions to ask regarding an agency's sexual abuse policy for inmates:

SEXUAL ABUSE POLICY CHECKLIST	YES	NO
Does the agency policy prohibit the sexual abuse of inmates or residents in custody?		
Does the agency policy stipulate that staff must receive training regarding the sexuality and sexual behaviors of inmates or residents?		
Does the agency policy require the investigation of all reports of violations of policy regarding sexual abuse?		
Does the agency have multiple methods for inmates or residents to report sexual abuse, including avenues for third-party, independent reporting?		
Does the agency policy address the management of inmates or residents who report allegations of sexual abuse?		
Do the agency inmate or resident disciplinary procedures address discipline for those who have sustained violations of recanting previous allegations?		
Does the agency policy define the roles and responsibilities of the investigative process into allegations of sexual abuse?		
Does the agency policy (or the investigative entity's policy) require referral of allegations of potential criminal activity for review by the prosecutor?		
Does the agency policy require a review of reports and investigations of sexual abuse?		
Does the agency policy establish a sexual assault response team?		
Do the agency protocols provide for ongoing medical and mental health care for an inmate or resident who has been sexually victimized while in custody?		
Does the agency policy recognize particularly vulnerable populations, such as LGBTI inmates or residents, and specify treatment for them?		

In correctional settings, there is a continuum of sexual behaviors that may include nonabusive or abusive sexual contact. It is important that agencies recognize this continuum of sexual behaviors in custody, have policies that reflect the continuum, and pay special attention to the increased vulnerability of LGBTI inmates or residents.

Endnotes

1. *See, e.g.,* Crime & Justice Inst. & Nat'l Inst. of Corrs., Implementing Evidence Based Policy and Practice in Community Corrections (2nd ed. 2009); Susan W. Campbell & Larry S. Fischer, Staff Sexual Misconduct with Inmates, Policy Development Guide for Sheriffs and Jail Administrators (2002).

2. It Gets Better, itgetsbetter.org (last visited Jan 31., 2013) ("In September 2010, syndicated columnist and author Dan Savage created a YouTube video with his partner Terry Miller to inspire hope for young people facing harassment. In response to a number of students taking their own lives after being bullied in school, they wanted to create a personal way for supporters everywhere to tell LGBT youth that, yes, it does indeed get better.").

3. Advancement Project, et al., Two Wrongs Don't Make a Right, Why Zero Tolerance is Not the Solution to Bullying (2012), *http://b.3cdn.net/advancement/73b640051a1066d43d_yzm6rkffb.pdf.*

4. *Id.*

5. Department of Justice, Statement of the Attorney General on Litigation Involving the Defense of Marriage Act, (Feb. 23, 2011), available at *http://www.justice.gov/opa/pr/2011/February/11-ag-222.html.*

6. *Election 2012 Shows A Social Sea Change On Gay Marriage,* Huffington Post, (Nov. 8, 2012), *http://www. huffingtonpost.com/2012/11/08/election-2012-gay-marriage-sea-change_n_2090106.html.*

7. *Minnesota Amendment 1 Same-Sex Marriage Ballot Measure Fails,* Huffington Post (Nov. 7, 2011), *http://www. huffingtonpost.com/2012/11/07/minnesota-amendment-1-results-2012_n_2050310.html.*

8. Emmanuela Grinberg, *Wisconsin's Tammy Baldwin is first openly gay person elected to Senate,* CNN (Nov. 7, 2011), *http://www.cnn.com/2012/11/07/politics/wisconsin-tammy-baldwin-senate/index.html.*

9. *See generally* National Institute of Corrections and the Center for Innovative Public Policy, Inc., Working with Lesbian, Gay, Bisexual, Transgender, and Intersex Populations in Corrections Systems: Identification of Issues and Resources, Development of Recommendations (2007) (unpublished document on file with the author).

10. Israel & Tarver, *supra* note 19 at 134-35; American Medical Association, Resolution 122: Removing Financial Barriers to Care for Transgender Patients (2008), *available at http://www.tgender.net/taw/ama_resolutions.pdf* [hereinafter AMA Resolution 122].

11. American Psychiatric Association, Diagnostic and Statistical Manual of Mental Disorders 576, 581 (4th ed., text revision 2000) (diagnostic criteria for GID include a persistent discomfort with one's assigned sex and with one's primary and secondary sex characteristics, which causes intense emotional pain and suffering).

12. Dani Heffernan, *The APA Removes "Gender Identity Disorder" From Updated Mental Health Guide,* GLAAD, (Dec. 3, 2012), *http://www.glaad.org/blog/apa-removes-gender-identity-disorder-updated-mental-health-guide.*

13. Often intersex conditions are called "disorders." There is a robust discussion in both the medical and advocacy communities about the use of the term. *See, e.g.,* Elizabeth Reis, *Divergence or Disorder: The Politics of Naming Intersex,* 50 Perspectives in Biology & Med. 535 (2007).

14. *See* Advocates for Informed Choice: FAQ, *http://aiclegal.org/faq/* (last visited Sept. 20, 2012). For more information about intersex conditions, visit Accord Alliance, *http://www.accordalliance.org.*

15. *See* Intersex Society of North America, *http://www.isna.org/faq/frequency* (last visited Sept. 20, 2012).

16. *E.g.,* 28 C.F.R. § 115.41 (2012).

17. 28 C.F.R. § 115.5 (2012).

18. According to studies, many youth report awareness of their sexual orientation by age five. Caitlyn Ryan & Rafael M. Diaz, *Family Responses as a Source of Risk and Resiliency for LGBTI Youth,* presentation at the pre-conference Institute on LGBTIQ Youth, Child Welfare League of America 2005 National Conference, Washington, D.C. (2005). Similarly, research indicates that a person's gender identity is firmly established by age three. Gerald P. Mallon & Teresa DeCrescenzo, *Transgender Children and Youth: A Child Welfare Practice Perspective,* 85 Child Welfare 215, 218 (2006); Shannan Wilber et al., Best Practice Guidelines for Serving LGBT Youth in Out of Home Care, Child Welfare League of America 2 (2006). It is not uncommon for pre-school aged children to self-identify as transgender. Stephanie Brill & Rachel Pepper, The Transgender Child: A Handbook for Families and Professionals 16-17 (Cleis Press Inc. 2008).

19. Brill & Pepper, *supra* note 15, at 16-17.

20. Caitlyn Ryan, *LGBTI Youth: Health Concerns, Services and Care,* 20 Clinical Res. & Reg. Affairs 137, 139 (2003) (*internal citations omitted*).

21. *See id.*

22. Gianna E. Israel & Donald E. Tarver II, Transgender Care: Recommended Guidelines, Practical Information, and Personal Accounts 134-5 (Temple University Press 1997); Gerald P. Mallon, Practice with Transgendered Children, in Social Services with Transgendered Youth 49, 55-6 (Gerald P. Mallon, ed., 1999); Barbara Bradley Hagerty, *Evangelicals Fight Over Therapy To 'Cure' Gays,* NPR (Jul. 6, 2012), *http://www.npr.org/2012/07/06/156367287/evangelicals-fight-over-therapy-to-cure-gays* (arguing conversion therapy makes people feel "sinful for their natural inclinations").

23. *See* American Psychological Association Task Force on Appropriate Therapeutic Responses to Sexual Orientation, Report of the Task Force on Appropriate Therapeutic Responses to Sexual Orientation 35-41(2009), *available at http://www.apa.org/pi/lgbc/publications/therapeutic-response.pdf* [hereinafter Task Force Report on Therapeutic Responses]; American Psychological Association, APA Help Center: Sexual Orientation and Homosexuality 1 (2009) *http://www.apa.org/helpcenter/sexual-orientation.aspx* (last visited Jan. 9, 2012) [hereinafter Sexual Orientation & Homosexuality].

24. *See* Task Force Report on Therapeutic Responses, *supra* note 13, at 2, 11; Sexual Orientation and Homosexuality, *supra* note 13; Gregory M. Herek & Linda D. Garnets, *Sexual Orientation and Mental Health,* 3 Ann. Rev. Clinical Psychol. 353, 359 (2007).

25. *See LGBT Sexual Orientation,* American Psychiatric Association (2011), *available at http://www.psychiatry.org/mental-health/people/lgbt-sexual-orientation* (According to the American Psychiatric Association, "sexual abuse does not appear to be more prevalent among children who grow up to identify as lesbian, gay, or bisexual than it does for their heterosexual counterparts.").

26. Collier M. Cole, Michael O'Boyle, Lee E. Emory, & Walther J. Meyer III, *Comorbidity of Gender Dysphoria and other Major Psychiatric Diagnoses,* 26 Archives of Sexual Behav. 13, 21 (1997) (citing three studies with similar findings completed over the span of 13 years); George R. Brown, *Transvestism and Gender Identity Disorder in Adults,* in Treatments of Psychiatric Disorders, 2034-35 (Glen O. Gabbard, M.D. ed., 3d ed. 2007).

27. WPATH is an international, multidisciplinary, professional organization whose mission is to promote evidence-based care, education, research, advocacy, public policy, and respect for transgender health. The organization's membership includes approximately hundreds of licensed professionals in the disciplines of medicine, psychiatry, nursing, psychology, sociology, social work, counseling, and law, from twenty countries, including the United States. The vision of WPATH is to bring together diverse professionals dedicated to developing best practices and supportive policies worldwide that promote health, research, education, respect, dignity, and equality for transsexual, transgender, and gender nonconforming people in all cultural settings. WPATH was formerly known as the Harry Benjamin International Gender Dysphoria Association, Inc. (HBIGDA). WPATH, *www.wpath.org* (last visited Sept. 28, 2012).

28. The World Professional Association for Transgender Health, The Standards of Care for the Health of Transsexual, Transgender, and Gender Nonconforming People (7th ed. 2011), *available at http://www.wpath.org/documents/Standards%20of%20Care%20V7%20-%202011%20WPATH.pdf* [hereinafter WPATH Standards of Care].

29. *See id.* at 8-9.

30. *Id.* at 8-10. These are examples of some of the types of medical care recommended for the treatment of gender dysphoria. Not all transgender people undergo medical treatments as part of transition. The actual treatment needs and the timing of treatment will depend on the individual person and can only be determined in collaboration with a qualified medical professional.

31. Mallon, *supra* note 19, at 51; Israel & Tarver, *supra* note 19, at 134-35; Brill & Pepper, *supra* note 15, at 74-75.

32. *See generally* WPATH Standards of Care, *supra* note 27 at 7; Walter O. Bockting & Eli Coleman, *A Comprehensive Approach to the Treatment of Gender Dysphoria*, in GID: Interdisciplinary Approaches in Clinical Management 131 (W.O. Bockting & E. Coleman eds., 1992); Wylie C. Hembree et al., *Endocrine Treatment of Transsexual Persons: An Endocrine Society Clinical Practice Guideline*, 94 J. of Clinical Endocrinology & Metabolism 3132, 3153-54 (2009); American Psychological Association, Transgender, Gender Identity, & Gender Expression Non-Discrimination 3 (2008), *available at http://www.apa.org/about/policy/transgender.aspx* [hereinafter APA Resolution]; AMA Resolution 122, *supra* note 24, at 2, n. 7.

33. AMA Resolution 122, *supra* note 24 at 1-2. *See generally* American Psychological Association Policy Statement, Transgender, Gender Identity, and Gender Expression Non-Discrimination (2008), *available at http://www.apa.org/about/policy/transgender.aspx* [hereinafter APA Transgender Statement].

34. *See* National Commission on Correctional Health Care, Position Statement on Transgender Health Care in Correctional Settings, (Oct. 18, 2009), *available at http://www.ncchc.org/transgender-health-care-in-correctional-settings;* APA Resolution, *supra* note 31.

35. Allen J. Beck & Candace Johnson, Bureau of Justice Statistics, NCJ 237363, Sexual Victimization Reported By Former State Prisoners, 2008 6 (2012), *available at http://bjs.ojp.usdoj.gov/content/pub/pdf/svrfsp08.pdf.*

36. Allen J. Beck, Paige Harrison, & Paul Guerino, Bureau of Justice Statistics, NCJ 228416, Sexual Victimization in Juvenile Facilities Reported by Youth, 2008–09 1 (2010), *available at bjs.ojp.usdoj.gov/content/pub/pdf/svjfry09.pdf.*

37. *See generally* Patricia Boland, *Vulnerability to Violence among Gay, Lesbian, and Bisexual Youth*, NASP Resources, *available at http://www.nasponline.org/resources/crisis_safety/neat_vulnerability.aspx.*

38. *Id.*

39. *See generally* Rebecca Cathcart, *Boy's Killing, Labeled a Hate Crime, Stuns Town*, N.Y. Times (Feb. 23, 2008), *available at http://www.nytimes.com/2008/02/23/us/23oxnard.html?_r=0.*

40. *See* Meg Earls, The Facts: GLBTQ Youth, Advocates for Youth (2005), *available at http://www.advocatesforyouth. org/storage/advfy/documents/fsglbt.pdf.*

41. *See generally Homeless Youth: Fact Sheet #13,* National Coalition for the Homeless (2008), *available at http:// www.nationalhomeless.org/publications/facts/youth.pdf* (last visited on Oct. 6, 2008).

42. *See generally* G. Kruks, *Gay and Lesbian Homeless/Street Youth: Special Issues and Concerns,* 12 J. of Adolescent Health 515 (1991).

43. Centers for Disease Control. "Lesbian, Gay, Bisexual and Transgender Health" (May 2011) *http://www.cdc.gov/ lgbthealth/youth.htm.*

44. *Id.*

45. Jerome Hunt and Aisha C. Moodie-Mills, "The Unfair Criminalization of Gay and Transgender Youth An Overview of the Experiences of LGBT Youth in the Juvenile Justice System," Center for American Progress (June 2012), *http://www. americanprogress.org/issues/lgbt/report/2012/06/29/11730/the-unfair-criminalization-of-gay-and-transgender- youth/.*

46. Jamie M. Grant, et al., Nat'l Center for Transgender Equal. & Nat'l Gay and Lesbian Task Force, Injustice at Every Turn: A Report of the National Transgender Discrimination Survey (2011).

47. *http://endtransdiscrimination.org/PDFs/BlackTransFactsheetFINAL_090811.pdf.*

48. *See* National Prison Rape Elimination Commission, Report 73-4 (June 2009) (hereinafter Commission Report) (citing W. S. Wooden & J. Parker, Men Behind Bars (De Capo Press 1982)); Valerie Jenness et al., Violence in California correctional facilities: An empirical examination of sexual assault (2009); *see generally,* Sylvia Rivera Law Project, It's War in Here: A Report on the Treatment of Transgender & Intersex People in New York State Men's Prisons (2007), *available at http://srlp.org/files/warinhere.pdf.*

49. Commission Report, *supra* note 49.

50. *See* National Prison Rape Elimination Commission, Executive Summary 7-9 (2009), *available at http://www.wcl. american.edu/endsilence/documents/NPREC_ExecSummary.pdf.*

51. *See id.*

52. Beck, Harrison & Guerino, *supra* note 37.

53. *See id.* at 11. In comparison, 11.1 percent of heterosexual youth reported such abuse. *Id.*

54. Beck & Johnson, *supra* note 36.

55. *Id.*

56. *See* Sylvia Rivera Law Project, *supra* note 41, at 17-19; Stop Prison Rape, In the Shadows: Sexual Violence in US Detention Facilities 14-15 (2006), *available at http://www.justdetention.org/pdf/in_the_shadows.pdf;* Stop Prison Rape & ACLU National Prison Project, Still in Danger: The Ongoing Threat of Sexual Violence Against Transgender People 5 (2005), *available at http://www.justdetention.org/pdf/stillindanger.pdf.*

57. *See* Jenness, *supra* note 49, at 30.

58. *Id.* at 29-30.

59. *See* Lori Sexton, Valerie Jenness & Jennifer Macy Sumner, *Where the Margins Meet: A Demographic Assessment of Transgender Offenders in Men's Prisons,* 27 Justice Quarterly 6, 858 (2010), *available at http://www.tandfonline.com/doi/pdf/10.1080/07418820903419010.*

60. *See generally* APA Transgender Statement, *supra* note 32. *See* National Commission of Correctional Health Care, Position Statement: Transgender Health Care in Correctional Settings (2009), *available at http://www.ncchc.org/transgender-health-care-in-correctional-settings.*

61. *See* The Equity Project, Hidden Injustice: Lesbian, Gay, Bisexual and Transgender Youth in Juvenile Courts 102-03 (2009), *available at http://www.equityproject.org/pdfs/hidden_injustice.pdf.*

62. Commission Report, *supra* note 49, at 74.

63. *See generally id.*

64. *Id.*

65. *Id.* at 7.

66. *Id.* at 73-74.

67. *Id.* at 73.

68. 28 C.F.R. § 115.5; 115.41 (2012).

69. *See* Joan W, Howarth, *Note, The Rights of Gay Prisoners: A Challenge to Protective Custody,* 53 S. Cal. L. Rev. 1225 (1980); Darren Rosenblum, *"Trapped" in Sing Sing: Transgendered Prisoners Caught in the Gender Binarism,* 6 Mich. J. Gender & L. 499, 530 (2000).

70. 28 C.F.R. § 115.43(a) (2012).

71. Paul Von Zielbauer, *City Prepares to Close Rikers Housing for Gays,* N.Y. Times (Dec. 30, 2005), *available at http://query.nytimes.com/gst/fullpage.html?res=9E0DE1D81330F933A05751C1A9639C8B63.*

72. The Equity Project, *supra* note 64 (detailing the collaboration between Legal Services for Children (LSC), the National Juvenile Defender Center (NJDC) and National Center for Lesbian Rights (NCLR)).

73. *Id.* at 127.

74. *Id.* at 111-12.

75. Angela Irvine, *"We've Had Three of Them": Addressing the Invisibility of Lesbian, Gay, Bisexual and Gender Non-Conforming Youths in the Juvenile Justice System,* 19 Colum. J. Gender & L. 675 (2010).

76. *See* Jody Marksamer, *And by the Way, Do You Know He Thinks He's a Girl? The Failures of Law, Policy, and Legal Representation for Transgender Youth in Delinquency Courts,* 5:1 Sexuality Res. & Soc. Pol'y 72, 82 (2008), *available at http://www.nclrights.org/site/DocServer/And_by_the_way_article.pdf?docID=3121;* The Equity Project, *supra* note 64, at 108-10.

77. *See* Marksamer, *supra* note 80, at 81; Equity Project, *supra* note 64, at 111-12; Complaint at 2-3, 6, *Rodriguez v. Johnson,* No. 06CV00214 (S.D.N.Y. filed Jan. 11, 2006) (on file with author).

78. *See Kent v. United States,* 383 U.S. 541, 554 (1966) ("The theory of the District's Juvenile Court Act, like that of other jurisdictions, is rooted in social welfare philosophy rather than in the corpus juris. Its proceedings are designated as civil rather than criminal."); *see also Ingraham v. Wright,* 430 U.S. 651, 671-72 n. 40 (1977) ("Eighth Amendment scrutiny is appropriate only after the state has complied with the constitutional guarantees traditionally associated with criminal prosecutions.") (internal citations omitted).

79. The First, Third, Fourth, Eighth, Ninth, Tenth, and Eleventh Circuit Courts have held that the appropriate standard to use in reviewing the conditions at juvenile facilities comes from the Due Process Clause of the Fourteenth Amendment, not from the Eighth Amendment. *See e.g., A.M.. v. Luzerne Cnty. Juvenile Det. Ctr.,* 372 F.3d 572 (3rd Cir. 2004) (finding appropriate standard for juvenile abused in detention was Fourteenth amendment due process, rather than Eighth amendment); *Alexander S.,* 876 F. Supp. 773, 782 (D.S.C. 1995), *aff'd in part and rev'd in part on other grounds,* 113 F.3d 1373 (4th Cir. 1997), *cert. denied,* 118 S.Ct. 880 (1998) (adopting the Fourteenth Amendment as the appropriate standard for evaluating juvenile conditions of confinement); *A.J. v. Kierst,* 56 F.3d 849, 854 (8th Cir. 1995) (agreeing that Due Process Clause of Fourteenth Amendment governs evaluation of conditions for confined juveniles); *Gary H. v. Hegstrom,* 831 F.2d 1430, 1431-32 (9th Cir. 1987) (resolving split in authorities by selecting Fourteenth Amendment standard instead of Eighth Amendment standard); *H.C. ex rel. Hewett v. Jarrard,* 786 F.2d 1080, 1084-85 (11th Cir. 1986) (noting conditions of confinement for juveniles affect liberty interests protected by the Fourteenth Amendment); *Santana v. Collazo,* 714 F.2d 1172, 1179 (1st Cir. 1983) (stating juveniles not convicted of crimes maintain due process interest in their liberty); *Milonas v. Williams,* 691 F.2d 931, 942, n. 10 (10th Cir. 1982) (noting confined juveniles maintain due process liberty interests). *But see Nelson v. Heyne,* 491 F.2d 352, 355 (7th Cir. 1974) (applying the cruel and unusual punishment test of the Eighth Amendment). The United States Supreme Court has not yet decided the issue.

80. *See A.M.,* 372 F.3d at 579 (acknowledging detained youth had liberty interest in personal security and well-being under the Fourteenth Amendment); *Alexander S.,* 876 F. Supp. at 782 ("[J]uveniles possess a clearly recognized liberty interest in being free from unreasonable threats to their physical safety."); *Milonas,* 691 F.2d at 942, n. 10 ("[B] ecause the state has no legitimate interest in punishment, the conditions of juvenile confinement...are subject to more exacting scrutiny than conditions imposed on convicted criminals.").

81. *See generally R.G. v. Koller,* 415 F. Supp. 2d 1129, 1133 (D. Haw. 2006).

82. *Id.*

83. *Id.* at 1162; *A.M.,* 372 F.3d at 581, 583.

84. *See, e.g., Koller,* 415 F. Supp. 2d at 1158 (finding placing vulnerable LGBTI youth in unit with aggressive boys amounts to deliberate indifference); *A.M.,* 372 F.3d at 579. (finding sufficient evidence individuals were deliberately indifferent to the substantial risk of harm to 13 year old boy with mental illness who was placed in general population).

85. *See Alexander S.,* 876 F. Supp. at 797- 98 (facilities must have a system for screening and separating aggressive juveniles from vulnerable juveniles); *Koller,* 415 F. Supp. 2d at 1158 (same).

86. *E.g., H.C. by Hewett v. Jarrard,* 786 F.2d 1080, 1088 (11th Cir. 1986) (juvenile isolated for seven days was entitled to damages for violation of 14th Amendment); *Santana v. Collazo,* 714 F.2d 1172 (1st Cir. 1983); *Milonas,* 691 F.2d at 942-43 (use of isolation rooms for periods less than 24 hours violated the 14th Amendment); *D.B. v. Tewksbury,* 545 F. Supp. 896, 905 (D.Or.1982); *Feliciano v. Barcelo,* 497 F. Supp. 14, 35 (D.P.R. 1979); *Morales v. Turman,* 364 F. Supp. 166 (E.D. Tex. 1973) (solitary confinement of young adults held unconstitutional); *Offenders of Boys' Training Sch. v. Affleck,* 346 F. Supp. 1354 (D.R.I. 1972); *Lollis v. N.Y. State Dep't of Soc. Servs.,* 322 F. Supp. 473, 480 (S.D.N.Y. 1970).

87. Youth in juvenile detention or correctional facilities should not be placed in conditions that amount to punishment or be stigmatized or humiliated as part of their treatment. With the understanding that some restrictions of liberty may be constitutional, a court will look at whether a particular restriction is "reasonably related" to a legitimate governmental interest to determine if there is a violation. If it is not, it may be inferred that the purpose of the restriction is punishment. *Bell v. Wolfish,* 441 U.S. 520, 539 (1979), *see also Milonas,* 691 F.2d at 942 ("Any institutional rules that amount to punishment of those involuntarily confined ...are violative of the due process clause per se.").

88. *Koller*, 415 F. Supp. 2d at 1156.

89. *Id.*

90. *Id.* at 1162; A.M., 372 F.3d at 581, 583.

91. For adults, courts have found that the classification of a prisoner as a "sex offender" has such stigmatizing consequences that unless the prisoner has a sexual offense history, additional constitutional protections must be met before this classification can take place. *See Neal* v. *Shimoda*, 131 F.3d 818, 830 (9th Cir. 1997) ("We can hardly conceive of a state's action bearing more 'stigmatizing consequences' than the labeling of a prison inmate as a sex offender."). Confined juveniles receive greater constitutional protections than adult inmates. Therefore, branding a juvenile with a sex offender label clearly would have the same, if not an even greater, stigmatizing effect.

92. *See Youngberg* v. *Romeo*, 457 U.S. 307 (1982); *Burton* v. *Richmond*, 276 F.3d 973 (8th Cir. 2002); *A.M.*, 372 F.3d at 585 n.3; *Jackson* v. *Johnson*, 118 F. Supp. 2d 278 at 289; *Alexander S.*, 876 F. Supp. at 788.

93. *See, e.g., A.M.* v. *Luzerne Cnty. Juvenile Det. Ctr.*, 372 F.3d 572, 584-85 (3rd Cir. 2004) (discussing lack of medical and mental health care forward with mental illness); *Jackson* v. *Johnson*, 118 F. Supp. 2d at 289; *Alexander S.*, 876 F. Supp. 773, 788 (D.S.C. 1995), *aff'd in part and rev'd in part on other grounds*, 113 F.3d 1373 (4th Cir. 1997).

94. Juvenile justice professionals must provide some form of appropriate treatment for transgender youth diagnosed with gender dysphoria. Even under the more restrictive minimally adequate medical care standard applicable to adults, courts have held that "transsexualism" constitutes a "serious medical need" therefore, deliberately denying access to transgender-related health care for people amounts to cruel and unusual punishment under the Eighth Amendment of the U.S. Constitution. *See, e.g., Allard* v. *Gomez*, 9 Fed. Appx. 793 (9th Cir. 2001); *Meriwether* v. *Faulkner*, 821 F.2d 408, 413 (7th Cir. 1987) (holding that "[t]here is no reason to treat transsexualism differently from any other psychiatric disorder"); *Kosilek* v. *Malone*, 221 F. Supp. 2d 156 (Mass. Dist. Ct. 2001); *Wolfe* v. *Horne*, 130 F. Supp. 2d 648 (E.D. Pa. 2001); *Phillips* v. *Michigan Dep't. of Corr.*, 731 F. Supp. 792 (W.D. Mich. 1990).

95. *See Henkle* v. *Gregory*, 150 F. Supp. 2d 1067, 1078 (D. Nev. 2001) (permitting claims under Title IX for discrimination and harassment by other students and under First Amendment based on demands by school officials that student keep his sexual orientation to himself to proceed through summary judgment).

96. *See, e.g., Doe* v. *Yunits*, No. 001060A, 2000 WL 33162199 (Mass. Super. Oct. 11,2000), *aff'd sub nom. Doe* v. *Brockton Sch. Comm.*, No. 2000-J-638, 2000 WL 33342399 (Mass. App. Ct. Nov. 30, 2000) (transgender student had First Amendment right to wear clothing consistent with her gender identity and that treating transgender girl differently than biological girls was discrimination on the basis of sex).

97. While First Amendment case law in the juvenile justice context is limited, in the public school context, courts have held school officials liable for forcing LGBTI youth to conceal their sexual orientation as a condition of enrollment, for not permitting a transgender student to dress in accordance with her gender identity, and for prohibiting students from bringing a same-sex date to the high school prom. These cases illustrate the types of violations that may be actionable for youth in the juvenile justice context. *LaShonda D.* v. *Monroe Cnty. Bd. of Educ.*, 526 U.S. 629 (1999); *Ray* v. *Antioch Unified Sch. Dist.*, 107 F. Supp. 2d 1165 (N.D. Cal. 2000); *Yunits*, 2000 WL 33162199 at *3; *Fricke* v. *Lynch*, 491 F. Supp. 387 (D.R.I. 1980).

98. *See Canell* v. *Lightner*, 143 F.3d 1210, 1214 (9th Cir. 1998) (finding a violation of the Establishment Clause if a plaintiff could make a factual showing that a facility condoned or ignored religious proselytizing by prison staff.).

99. *See R.G.* v. *Koller*, 415 F. Supp. 2d 1129, 1160-61 (D. Haw. 2006) ("[T]he court is concerned by the evidence that members of the HYCF staff have promoted certain religious teachings to the plaintiffs.").

100. Barbara Bradley Hagerty, *Evangelicals Fight Over Therapy To 'Cure' Gays*, NPR (Jul. 6, 2012), *http://www.npr.org/2012/07/06/156367287/evangelicals-fight-over-therapy-to-cure-gays*.

101. *Id.*

102. *Id.*

103. West's Ann. Cal. Bus. & Prof. Code § 865.1.

104. West's Ann. Cal. Bus. & Prof. Code § 865.2.

105. *Compare Welch* v. *Brown,* No. CIV 2:12-2484 WBS KJN (E.D. Cal., Dec. 3, 2012) (finding that the statute was subject to strict scrutiny and issuing preliminary injunction barring its enforcement against the plaintiffs), *with Pickup* v. *Brown,* No. 2:12-CV-02497-KJM-EFB (E.D. Cal., Dec. 4, 2012) (holding found that the statute was subject to rationality review, and denying a preliminary injunction).

106. 28 C.F.R. § (115.341)(c)(2).

107. 28 C.F.R. § (115.341)(c)(10).

108. 28 C.F.R. § (115.341)(c)(11).

109. 28 C.F.R. § (115.342)(c).

110. 28 C.F.R. § (115.342)(f).

111. 28 C.F.R. § (115.342)(g).

112. 28 C.F.R. § (115.342)(e).

113. 28 C.F.R. § (115.342)(h)(1-2).

114. 28 C.F.R. § (115.342)(i).

115. 28 C.F.R. § (115.315)(f).

116. 28 C.F.R. § (115.315)(e).

117. 28 C.F.R. § (115.341)(a)(9).

118. 28 C.F.R. § (115.378)(g).

119. 28 C.F.R. § (115.386)(d)(2).

120. SB 518 Jan 2008 [prohibits harassment and discrimination based on actual or perceived race, ethnic group identification, ancestry, national origin, color, religion, sex, sexual orientation, gender identity, mental or physical disability, and HIV status in all California Department of Juvenile Justice (DJJ) facilities]; R.I. Gen. Laws § 28-5.1-7 (a) [Every state agency shall render service to the citizens of this state without discrimination based on race, color, religion, sex, sexual orientation, gender identity or expression, age, national origin, or disability. No state facility shall be used in furtherance of any discriminatory practice nor shall any state agency become a party to any agreement, arrangement, or plan which has the effect of sanctioning those patterns or practices]; Minn. Stat. § 363A.02 (4) [prohibits discrimination in public services based on race, color, creed, religion, national origin, sex, marital status, disability, sexual orientation, and status with regard to public assistance.]; Iowa Code Ann. § 19B.12 (2) [prohibiting "state employees from discriminating against a person in the care or custody of the employee or a state institution based on sex."]; *See, e.g., Chisolm* v. *McManimom,* 275 F.3d 315, 325 (adult jail, like a hospital, is place of public accommodation under New Jersey's Law Against Discrimination); *Ortland* v. *County of Tehama,* 939 F. Supp. 1465,

1470 (California Unruh Act is applicable in claims against governmental agencies); *Doe v. Bell,* 754 N.Y.S.2d 846, 850 (N.Y. Sup. Ct. 2003) (recognizing residential foster care facility as "publicly-assisted housing accommodation" for purposes of disability discrimination claim under New York's Human Rights Law).

121. National Juvenile Detention Association, Code of Ethics, 3 (2009), *available at npjs.org/wp-content/ uploads/2013/01/NPJS-Code-of-Ethics.pdf;* American Correctional Association, Code of Ethics (1994), *http://www. aca.org/pastpresentfuture/ethics.asp.*

122. National Juvenile Detention Association, *supra* note 128; See also *A.M. v. Luzerne Cnty. Juvenile Det. Ctr.,* 372 F.3d 572, 583 (3rd Cir. 2004) (finding that failure to follow up on grievance reports contributes to a finding of liability based on deliberate indifference); R.G. v. Koller, 415 F. Supp. 2d 1129, 1158 (D. Haw. 2006) (same).

123. Developed by SME group. *See supra* p. 11-13.

124. *Alexander S.,* 876 F. Supp. at 798; R.G., 415 F. Supp. 2d at 1152.

125. *Bell v. Wolfish,* 441 U.S. 520, 539 (1979); *see also Milonas v. Williams,* 691 F.2d 931, 942 (10th Cir. 1982) ("any institutional rules that amount to punishment of those involuntarily confined ... are violative of the due process clause per se").

126. *See* Hidden Injustice, *supra* note 55, at 106 -107.

127. For adults, courts have found that the classification of a prisoner as a "sex offender" has such stigmatizing consequences that unless the prisoner has a sexual offense history, additional constitutional protections must be met before this classification can take place. *See Neal v. Shimoda,* 131 F.3d 818, 830 (9th Cir. 1997) ("We can hardly conceive of a state's action bearing more 'stigmatizing consequences' than the labeling of a prison inmate as a sex offender."). Confined juveniles receive greater constitutional protections than adult inmates. Therefore, branding a juvenile with a sex offender label clearly would have the same, if not an even greater, stigmatizing effect.

128. 28 C.F.R. § (115.342)(c) (2012).

129. 28 C.F.R. § (115.342)(c).

130. NY OCFS, HYCF, Santa Clara County, DC juvenile facilities all have specific policies that speak to housing of TG youth in juvenile facilities.

131. 28 C.F.R. § 115.342)(g).

132. Adults who are in pre-trial detention and have not been convicted of a crime are entitled to the higher level of protection that is provided to juveniles in facilities under the Fourteenth Amendment Due Process Clause. Adults in pre-trial detention should not be placed in conditions that amount to punishment or be stigmatized or humiliated while detained. *See Bell v. Wolfish,* 441 U.S. 520. 539 (1982).

133. *See Farmer v. Brennan,* 511 U.S. 825 (1994) (explaining prison officials permitting the beating or rape of one person by another serves no legitimate penological objective and is outside of evolving standards of decency).

134. *Id.* at 843.

135. *Id.*

136. *See, e.g., Taylor v. Michigan Dep't of Corr.,* 69 F.3d 76, 87 (6th Cir. 1995) (knowledge of an inmate's "feminine mannerisms or homosexual orientation" put official on notice of risk of physical and sexual assault).

137. *See, e.g., Green v. Bowles,* 361 F.3d 290, 294-95 (6th Cir. 2004) (transsexual victim had raised a triable issue of fact as to deliberate indifference "because of her status as a vulnerable offender"); *Johnson v. Johnson,* 385 F.3d 503,

527 (5th Cir. 2004) (finding a deliberate indifference claim where prison officials continued to house a gay person in the general population where he was gang raped and sold as a sexual slave for over 18 months).

138. *Green*, 361 F.3d at 294.

139. *See Estate of DiMarco v. Wyoming Dept. of Corr.*, 473 F.3d 1334, 1342-43 (10th Cir. 2007) (finding segregation of person with an intersex condition was permissible because it was primarily to protect her; the prison had not previously dealt with an intersex person; alternatives such as transfer were impracticable; person was not denied access to all programs or services; and her segregation was regularly and meaningfully reviewed); *Meriwether v. Faulkner*, 821 F.2d 408, 416 (7th Cir. 1987); *Farmer v. Carlson*, 685 F. Supp. 1335 (D. MD 1988) (finding temporary segregation of transgender person awaiting transfer to another facility was not unconstitutional).

140. *Murray v. U.S. Bureau of Prisons*, 106 F.3d 401, *2 (6th Cir. 1997) (table of unreported decisions).

141. *Estelle v. Gamble*, 429 U.S. 97 (1976).

142. *Long v. Nix*, 877 F. Supp. 1358 (S.D. Iowa 1995).

143. *See, e.g., Cuoco v. Moritsugu*, 222 F.3d 99, 106 (2d Cir. 2000) (assuming without deciding that GID presents a serious medical need); *De'Lonta v. Angelone*, 330 F.3d 630, 634 (4th Cir. 2003); *Praylor v. Texas Dept. of Criminal Justice*, 430 F.3d 1208 (5th Cir. 2005) (assuming without deciding that GID presents a serious medical need); *Phillips v. Mich. Dept. of Corr.*, 932 F.2d 969 (6th Cir. 1991), aff'd. 731 F. Supp. 792 (W.D. Mich.1990); *Meriwether*, 821 F.2d at 413 (GID is "a very complex medical and psychological problem," there is "no reason to treat [GID] differently than any other psychiatric disorder."); *White v. Farrier*, 849 F.2d 322, 325-327 (8th Cir. 1988); *Allard v. Gomez*, 9 F. Appx. 793, 794 (9th Cir. 2001); *Brown v. Zavaras*, 63 F.3d 967, 970 (10th Cir. 1995). No circuit has held otherwise.

144. *E.g., Praylor v. Texas Dept. of Criminal Justice*, 430 F.3d 1208 (5th Cir. 2005) (denying relief because of absence of evidence of medical necessity in inmate's specific case); *Murray*, 106 F.3d at 401 (refusing to second-guess appropriateness of hormone dosage levels determined by physician); *See, e.g., De'Lonta*, 330 F.3d at 635 (finding that the Prozac prescribed to the plaintiff was not clearly provided to her for the purpose of treating GID needs, nor was it a reasonable method for addressing these needs); *Kosilek v. Maloney*, 221 F. Supp. 2d 156, 188 (D. Mass. 2002) (concluding that pharmacological evaluation does not constitute treatment for plaintiff's GID).

145. *Allard v. Gomez*, 9 Fed. Appx. 793, 795 (9th Cir. 2001) (holding that denial of medical care based on a blanket rule constitutes deliberate indifference).

146. *Kosilek v. Maloney*, 221 F. Supp. 2d 156, 162 (D. Mass. 2002).

147. *Young v. Adams*, 693 F. Supp. 2d 635, 641 (W.D. Tex. 2010).

148. *Fields*, 2011 WL 3436875, at *7 (quoting district court). *See also Barrett v. Coplan*, 292 F. Supp. 2d 281, 286 (D. N.H. 2003) (holding plaintiff stated claims upon which relief may be granted by alleging defendants denied her medical care based on a policy that prohibited hormone treatment for GID); *Houston v. Trella*, No. 04-CV-1393, 2006 WL 2772748 at 8 (D.N.J. Sept. 25, 2006) (holding that plaintiff in immigration detention has a viable claim if decision to deny hormone therapy was based on a non-medical reason such as an existing policy); *Kosilek*, 221 F. Supp. 2d at186 (D. Mass. 2002) (finding policy that precludes possibility that plaintiff will ever have hormone treatment initiated, when hormone treatment is a professionally recognized form of treatment that may be necessary for people diagnosed with GID, may be found to violate the Eighth Amendment).

149. *Brooks v. Berg*, 270 F. Supp. 2d 302 (N.D.N.Y. 2003), vacated in part on other grounds, 289 F. Supp. 2d 286 (N.D.N.Y. 2003). Two courts have found that such "freeze-frame" policies do not amount to a violation of Equal Protection. *See Oz'etax v. Ortiz*, 170 Fed. Appx. 551 (10th Cir. 2006); *Farmer v. Hawk-Sawyer*, 69 F. Supp. 2d 120

(D.D.C. 1999). These cases have no bearing on prisons' duty to provide adequate medical care for inmates with GID under the Eighth Amendment.

150. *Barrett*, 292 F. Supp. 2d at 286 (finding plaintiff asserted sufficient facts to state a claim based on prison not prescribing any of the treatments enumerated in the professionally recognized standards of care for GID); *Kosilek*, 221 F. Supp. 2d at 161, 167 (finding that because plaintiff was only seen by social worker and psychiatrist who did not have experience diagnosing GID, "qualified physicians have never evaluated" plaintiff and thus there was no individualized medical evaluation).

151. *See, e.g., Kosilek*, 221 F. Supp. 2d at 191; *Tates v. Blanas*, No. S-00-2539, 2003 WL 23864868, *10 (E.D. Cal. Mar. 11, 2003) (officials could not deny transgender woman a bra where they failed to balance security risks against medical needs, and where other women were issued bras); *Battista v. Clarke*, 645 F.3d 449 (1st Cir. 2011) (security considerations matter at prisons; as such, administrators have to balance conflicting demands and ensure that judgments are within the realm of reason and are made in good faith).

152. *Kosilek*, 221 F. Supp. 2d at 182.

153. *See Konitzer v. Frank*, 711 F. Supp. 2d 874 (E.D. Wis. 2010) (holding that prison officials' denial of plaintiff's requests for makeup, women's undergarments, and facial hair remover might give rise to an Eighth Amendment violation for deliberate indifference to a serious medical need, given that such elements of expression/presentation were part of the "real life experience" prescribed by the Standards of Care).

154. *See generally* WPATH Standards of Care, *supra* note 20.

155. *Konitzer*, 711 F. Supp. 2d at 874; *Kosilek*, 221 F. Supp. 2d at 167. The medical necessity of Real Life Experience is distinct from inmates' First Amendment interest in expressing their gender identity. Courts have held in other contexts that a person's expression of his or her core gender identity through dress and grooming is protected by the First Amendment. *Doe v. Yunits*, No. 001060A, 2000 WL 33162199 (Mass. Super. Oct. 11, 2000), aff'd, 2000 WL 33342399 (Mass. Appl. Ct. Nov. 30, 2000); *Logan v. Gary Community School Corp.*, No. 2:07-CV-431, 2008 WL 4411518 (N.D. Ind. Sept. 25, 2008). Other courts have held that in the prison context these expressive interests can be curtailed for a legitimate penological purpose. *Turner v. Safley*, 482 U.S. 78 (1987).

156. *Lamb v. Maschner*, 633 F. Supp. 351 (D. Kan. 1986).

157. *Kosilek*, 221 F. Supp. 2d at 874.

158. *Kosilek v. Spencer*, --- F. Supp. 2d ----, 2012 WL 4054248 (D. Mass. Sept. 16, 2012).

159. *De'Lonta v. Johnson*, 2011 WL 5157262 (W.D. Va. Oct. 28, 2011).

160. *De'Lonta v. Johnson*, --- F.3d ----, 2013 WL 310350 (4th Cir. 2013).

161. *Farmer v. Perrill*, 288 F.3d 1254, 1260 (10th Cir. 2002) (emphasis in original) (transgender woman was regularly searched in full view of other inmates whenever she returned from the common area). Other courts are in accord. *Mays v. Springborn*, 575 F.3d 643 (7th Cir. 2009); *Hayes v. Marriott*, 70 F.3d 1144 (10th Cir. 1995); *Elliott v. Lynn*, 38 F.3d 188 (5th Cir. 1994); *Cornwell v. Dahlberg*, 963 F.2d 912 (6th Cir. 1992); *Franklin v. Lockhart*, 883 F.2d 654 (8th Cir. 1989); *Michenfelder v. Sumner*, 860 F.2d 328 (9th Cir. 1988).

162. 821 F.2d 408 (7th Cir. 1987).

163. *Id.*

164. *Doe v. Sparks*, 733 F. Supp. 227, 232-34 (W.D. Pa. 1990).

165. *Whitmire v. State of Arizona*, 298 F.3d 1134 (9th Cir. 2002).

166. *Visiting a Friend or Loved One in Prison*, California Department of Corrections and Rehabilitation 3, *http://www.cdcr.ca.gov/Visitors/docs/InmateVisitingGuidelines.pdf*.

167. Mississippi Department of Corrections, *http://www.mdoc.state.ms.us/conjugal_visits.htm* (last visited Jan 30, 2013).

168. *See, e.g., Phelps v. Dunn*, 965 F.2d 93, 100 (6th Cir. 1992) (holding that a genuine issue of material fact existed as to whether a gay person alleging he was denied permission to attend religious services was denied because he was gay).

169. *See, e.g., Kelley v. Vaughn*, 760 F. Supp. 161, 163-64 (W.D. Mo. 1991) (denying prison's motion to dismiss on the ground that a gay person, bringing an action against the prison's food service manager to challenge his removal from his job as bakery worker, might have a valid equal protection claim); *Johnson v. Knable*, 862 F.2d 314 (4th Cir. 1988) (vacating lower court's summary judgment dismissal of an equal protection claim brought by a gay person noting that "[i]f [the plaintiff] was denied a prison work assignment simply because of his sexual orientation, his equal protection rights may have been violated").

170. *See, e.g., Howard v. Cherish*, 575 F. Supp. 34, 36 (S.D.N.Y. 1983) (a gay person who claimed he was punished because he was gay would have had a claim under § 1983 if he had been able to show that he was discriminated against solely because of his sexual orientation).

171. *See Powell v. Shriver*, 175 F.3d 107 (2d Cir. 1999). *See also Doe v. Delie*, 257 F.3d 309, 317 (3d Cir. 2001) (holding that inmates have a privacy interest in HIV status).

172. *Powell*, 175 F.3d at 113-14.

173. *Thornburgh v. Abbott*, 490 U.S. 401, 109 S. Ct. 1874, 104 L. Ed. 2d 459 (1989).

174. *See, e.g., Mauro v. Arpaio*, 188 F.3d 1054, 1060 (9th Cir. 1999) (upholding regulations prohibiting people from possessing sexually explicit materials on grounds that regulation was "reasonably related to legitimate penological interests"); *Allen v. Wood*, 970 F. Supp. 824, 831 (E.D. Wash. 1997) (granting defendant prison's motion for summary judgment on ground that prison regulations prohibiting certain sexually explicit materials satisfied the reasonable relation standard).

175. 28 C.F.R. § 115.41(c)(7) (2012).

176. 28 C.F.R. § 115.41(g).

177. 28 C.F.R. § 115.42(g).

178. 28 C.F.R. § 115.42(g).

179. 28 C.F.R. § 115.42(c).

180. 28 C.F.R. § 115.42(e).

181. 28 C.F.R. § 115.42(d).

182. 28 C.F.R. § 115.15(e).

183. 28 C.F.R. § 115.15(d).

184. 28 C.F.R. § 115.15(e).

185. 28 C.F.R. § 115.31(a)(9).

186. 28 C.F.R. § 115.78(g).

187. 28 C.F.R. § 115.86(d)(2).

188. Lockup means a facility that contains holding cells, cell blocks, or other secure enclosures that are: (1) Under the control of a law enforcement, court, or custodial officer; and (2) Primarily used for the temporary confinement of individuals who have recently been arrested, detained, or are being transferred to or from a court, jail, prison, or other agency. 28 C.F.R. § 115.5.

189. 28 C.F.R. § 115.141(c).

190. 28 C.F.R. § 115.141(d)(3).

191. 28 C.F.R. § 115.15(d).

192. 28 C.F.R. § 115.115(d).

193. 28 C.F.R § 115.115(e).

194. 28 C.F.R. § 115.186(c)(2).

195. Community confinement facility means a community treatment center, halfway house, restitution center, mental health facility, alcohol or drug rehabilitation center, or other community correctional facility (including residential re-entry centers), other than a juvenile facility, in which individuals reside as part of a term of imprisonment or as a condition of pre-trial release or post-release supervision, while participating in gainful employment, employment search efforts, community service, vocational training, treatment, educational programs, or similar facility-approved programs during nonresidential hours. 28 C.F.R. § 115.5.

196. 28 C.F.R. § 115.241(d)(7).

197. 28 C.F.R. § 115.241(g).

198. 28 C.F.R. § 115.242(c).

199. 28 C.F.R. § 115.242(f).

200. 28 C.F.R. § 115.241(c).

201. 28 C.F.R. § 115.242(d).

202. 28 C.F.R. § 115.242(e).

203. 28 C.F.R. § 115.215(e).

204. 28 C.F.R. § 115.215(f).

205. 28 C.F.R. § 115.278(g).

206. 28 C.F.R. § 115.286(d)(2).

207. *See supra* note 110.

208. 28 C.F.R. § 115.41(c)(7).

Glossary

Asexual. A person who is not romantically or sexually attracted to any gender.

Bisexual. A person who is romantically or sexually attracted to more than one gender or sexual category.

Gender. A socially constructed concept classifying behavior as either "masculine" or "feminine," unrelated to one's external genitalia.

Gender expression. A person's expression of his/her gender identity, including appearance, dress, mannerisms, speech, and social interactions.

Gender identity. Distinct from sexual orientation and refers to a person's internal, deeply felt sense of being male or female.

Gender nonconforming. Gender characteristics and/or behaviors that do not conform to those typically associated with a person's biological sex.

Gender "norms." The expectations associated with "masculine" or "feminine" conduct, based on how society commonly believes males and females should behave.

Gender-variant behavior. Conduct that is not normatively associated with an individual's biological sex.

Heterosexual. Sexual or romantic attraction to a sex different from one's own.

Homosexuality. Sexual, emotional, and/or romantic attraction to a person of the same sex.

Intersex. An individual born with external genitalia, internal reproductive organs, chromosome patterns, and/or endocrine systems that do not seem to fit typical definitions of male or female.

LGBTI. Acronym for a group of sexual minorities, including lesbian, gay, bisexual, transgender, and intersex individuals.

Questioning. An active process in which a person explores his/her own sexual orientation and/or gender identity and questions the cultural assumptions that they are heterosexual and/or gender conforming.

Sex. An individual's anatomical makeup, including external genitalia, chromosomes, and reproductive system.

Sexual identity. The sex that a person sees themself as. This can include refusing to label oneself with a sex.

Sexual orientation. Romantic and/or physical attraction to members of the same or a different sex.

Transgender. A person whose gender identity differs from his/her birth sex.

Transgender female. A person whose birth sex was male but who understands herself to be, and desires to live her life as, a female.

Transgender male. A person whose birth sex was female but who understands himself to be, and desires to live his life as, a male.

Transsexual. An individual whose physical anatomy does not match his/her gender identity and who seeks medical treatment (sex reassignment surgery or hormones).

Transvestite. An individual who engages in gender-nonconforming behavior, such as adopting the gender expression of the opposite sex for purposes of sexual or emotional gratification, but does not necessarily consider his/her gender identity to be different from his/her sex.

Case Law Digest

Juvenile Case Law

Minimal Conditions for Confinement for Detained Lesbian, Gay, Bisexual, Transgender, and Intersex (LGBTI) Youth

R.G. v. *Koller,* 2006 WL 905225 (D. Hawaii Mar. 1, 2006) (preliminary injunction order)—Prohibiting the facility from discriminating against youth based on LGBTI status and using isolation to control the LGBTI population, and ordering the facility to develop policies and procedures for LGBTI youth.

Protection from Sexual Assault

A.M. v. *Luzerne County,* 372 F.3d 572 (3d Cir. 2004)—Finding that staff were deliberately indifferent to sexual assaults on youth in the detention facility.

Right to Medical and Rehabilitative Treatment under 14th Amendment

Farrell v. *Allen,* RG 03079344 (Superior Court of California Alameda County Nov. 19, 2004) (unpublished consent decree)—Developing a comprehensive plan to address severe problems within the California Youth Authority by implementing policies and procedures designed to provide appropriate medical and psychological treatment and rehabilitative care for all youth.

Bowers v. *Boyd,* 876 F. Supp. 773 (D.S.C. 1995)—Ordering the South Carolina Department of Juvenile Justice to develop policies and procedures to better protect youth in their custody.

Medical Treatment for Youth with Gender Identity Disorder

Complaint, *Rodriguez* v. *Johnson,* No. 06CV00214 (S.D.N.Y. filed Jan. 11, 2006)—Ending in a settlement agreement, wherein the New York State Office of Children and Family Services was required to implement a systemwide change to ensure treatment for transgender youth.

Segregation of LGBTI Youth

In re Antonie D, 137 Cal. App. 4th 1314 (Cal. App. 1 Dist.6 2006)—Permitting a bisexual juvenile detainee to challenge the juvenile court's refusal of his request to be placed in a facility that could better accommodate LGBTI youth.

Use of Isolation for Protection

R.G. v. *Koller,* 2006 WL 905225 (D. Hawaii Mar. 1, 2006) (preliminary injunction order)—Prohibiting the use of isolation to control the LGBTI population.

Housing Transgender Youth

R.G. v. *Koller*, 2006 WL 905225 (D. Hawaii Mar. 1, 2006) (preliminary injunction order)—Prohibiting the facility from discriminating against youth based on LGBTI status when making housing determinations.

Gender-Nonconforming Dressing Practices in Youth

Doe v. *Bell*, 754 N.Y.S.2d 846 (N.Y. Sup. 2003)—Recognizing that a juvenile detainee with gender identity disorder (GID) must be permitted to wear feminine clothing as part of her treatment, and finding the center's safety concerns underlying the policy prohibiting her from wearing feminine clothing was not a rational basis for rejecting the accommodation.

Doe v. *Yunits*, 2000 WL 33162199 (Mass. Super. Oct. 11, 2000)—Granting a preliminary injunction to a biologically male student with GID, permitting him to wear feminine clothing to his public high school.

Adult Case Law

Discrimination Based on Sexual Orientation under the 14th Amendment

Brown v. *Johnson*, 743 F.2d 408 (1984)—"Blanket ban against holding of group worship services by church which ministered to spiritual needs of homosexual persons was reasonably related to state's interest in maintaining internal security in prison, in view of undisputed testimony linking inmate homosexuality with prison violence."

Fitzpatrick v. *Curry*, 2006 WL 2990283 (W.D. Mich. Oct. 16, 2006)—Finding that a homosexual inmate could not sustain an Equal Protection claim against prison officials, as he was unable to establish that prison officials allowed the inmate to be raped due to his sexual orientation.

Protection from Sexual Assault under the Eighth Amendment

Farmer v. *Brennan*, 511 U.S. 825 (1970)—Establishing the standard of "deliberate indifference" to address claims brought by sexually abused inmates under the Eighth Amendment.

Johnson v. *Johnson*, 385 F.3d 503, 527 (5th Cir. 2004)—Finding a deliberate indifference claim where prison officials continued to house a gay person in the general population, where he was gang raped and sold as a sex slave for over 18 months.

Greene v. *Bowels*, 361 F.3d 290 (6th Cir. 2004)—Remanding an Eighth Amendment case brought by a preoperative male-to-female transsexual who was sexually assaulted while incarcerated in a male prison, to determine whether the warden knew of the risk presented by housing a transsexual inmate in the same unit with a predatory inmate.

Taylor v. *Michigan DOC*, 69 F.3d 76 (6th Cir. 1995)—Finding a triable issue of fact, where a mildly mentally retarded inmate with youthful looking features and a seizure disorder was raped in a prison, where the warden and his subordinates should have been aware of the dangerous conditions posed to vulnerable inmates.

Eighth Amendment Deliberate Indifference to Serious Medical Need for Treatment of Transgender Inmates Providing Continuing Hormonal Treatment

Fields v. *Smith*, 712 F. Supp. 2d 830 (E.D. Wis. 2010)—Holding that correctional officers violated inmate's 8th and 14th Amendment rights by enforcing a state statute preventing Department of Corrections medical personnel from providing hormone therapy or sex reassignment surgery to inmates with GID.

Maggert v. *Hanks,* 131 F.3d 670 (7th Cir. 1997)—Holding that absent special circumstances, inmates are not entitled to curative treatment for gender dysphoria under the Eighth Amendment.

Phillips v. *Michigan Dept. of Corrections,* 731 F. Supp. 792 (W.D. Mich. 1990)—Granting a preliminary injunction to an inmate with GID, ordering correctional officials to provide estrogen therapy.

De'Lonta v. *Angelone,* 330 F.3d 630 (4th Cir. 2003)—Permitting a transgender inmate who had engaged in self-mutilation to proceed in her claim that correctional officials who withdrew her hormone therapy were deliberately indifferent to her serious medical need.

Barrett v. *Coplan,* 292 F. Supp. 2d 281 (D.N.H. 2003)—Holding that an inmate with GID adequately stated a claim under the Eighth Amendment, where treatment was denied due to a policy that prohibited any hormone or surgical treatment for inmates suffering from GID.

Request for Hormonal Treatment Where Hormone Usage Does Not Pre-date Incarceration

Farmer v. *Moritsugu,* 163 F.3d 610 (D.C. Cir. 1998)—Finding that a Bureau of Prisons (BOP) medical director was entitled to qualified immunity from liability, where his denial of a transsexual prisoner's request for treatment aligned with constitutional BOP medical policy.

Lamb v. *Maschner,* 633 F. Supp. 351 (D. Kan. 1986)—Holding that an inmate did not have a constitutional right to transfer to a women's facility, to receive cosmetics and female clothing, or to receive hormone treatment or a sex-change operation.

Kosilek v. *Maloney,* 221 F. Supp. 2d 156 (D. Mass. 2002)—Stating that a treatment plan for an inmate with GID was inadequate to meet the inmate's serious medical need, as the treatment plan was made pursuant to a blanket policy prohibiting hormones that had not been prescribed prior to incarceration.

Brooks v. *Berg,* 270 F. Supp. 2d 302 (N.D. N.Y. 2003), *vacated in part on other grounds,* 289 F. Supp. 2d 286 (N.D. N.Y. 2003)—Recognizing that prison officials who failed to provide treatment to a transsexual inmate were deliberately indifferent to his serious medical needs, where the decision not to treat the inmate was not based on sound medical judgment.

Young v. *Adams,* 693 F. Supp. 2d 635 (W.D. Tex. 2010)—Finding that an inmate with GID was not entitled to receive hormone therapy.

Long v. *Nix,* 877 F. Supp. 1358 (S.D. Iowa 1995)—Holding that the denial of "desired accommodations and medical treatment" did not violate an inmate's 8th or 14th Amendment rights.

Gammett v. *Idaho State Board of Corrections,* 2007 WL 2186896 (D. Idaho Jul. 27, 2007)—Granting a preliminary injunction for a transsexual inmate who had castrated himself, ordering correctional officers to provide treatment for his GID.

Right to Sex Reassignment Surgery

De'Lonta v. *Johnson,* --- F.3d ----, 2013 WL 310350 (4th Cir. 2013)—Remanding case to lower court and requiring a hearing on the merits of a male-to-female transgender inmate's suit demanding that the Virginia Department of Corrections provide her with sex reassignment surgery.

Kosilek v. *Spencer,* --- F. Supp. 2d ----, 2012 WL 4054248 (D. Mass. Sept. 16, 2012)—Holding that a transsexual inmate displayed a serious medical need and was therefore entitled to sex reassignment surgery.

Right to Marry for All Inmates

Turner v. Safely, 482 U.S. 78 (1987)—Striking down a prison's marriage regulation prohibiting inmates from marrying other inmates or civilians without the prison superintendent's determination that there were compelling reasons for marriage.

Gerber v. Hickman, 291 F.3d 617 (9th Cir. 2002)—Finding that a prisoner had no federal or state constitutional right that would require the prison warden to allow the inmate to provide his wife with a sperm specimen for artificial insemination.

Bradbury v. Wainwright, 718 F.2d 1538 (11th Cir. 1983)—Permitting inmates to challenge the Florida Department of Corrections' administrative regulation restricting inmate marriage.

Segregation of Adult LGBTI Inmates

Estate of DiMarco v. Wyoming Dept. of Corr., 473 F.3d 1334, 1342-43 (10th Cir. 2007)—Finding that segregation of a person with an intersex condition was permissible because it was primarily to protect her, the prison had not previously dealt with an intersex person, alternatives such as transfer were impractical, the person was not denied access to all programs or services, and her segregation was regularly and meaningfully reviewed.

Gay Inmates of Shelby County v. Barksdale, 819 F.2d 289 (6th Cir. 1987)—Finding that an injunction ordering correctional officials to create an intake classification scheme to identify and house LGBTI inmates, rather than segregating LGBTI inmates, was an appropriate remedy.

Farmer v. Carlson, 685 F. Supp. 1335 (M.D. Pa. 1988)—Holding that prison officials did not violate a transsexual inmate's 8th or 14th Amendment rights by placing that inmate in administrative segregation for 4.5 months.

Strip Searches for Transgender Inmates Performed by Staff of the Same Biological Sex

Konitzer v. Frank, 711 F. Supp. 2d 874 (E.D. Wis. 2010)—Stating that prison officials were not required to ensure that strip searches of a biological male inmate suffering from GID be performed only by female officers.

Farmer v. Perrill, 288 F.3d 1254 (10th Cir. 2002)—Prohibiting prison officials from performing strip searches of a preoperative male-to-female transsexual in a humiliating fashion.

Visits with Partners

Whitmire v. Arizona, 298 F.3d 1134 (9th Cir. 2002)—Refusing to dismiss a homosexual partner's equal protection challenge to a prison regulation prohibiting same-sex kissing and hugging among nonfamily members during prison visits, in the absence of evidence proving a rational connection between the visitation policy and correctional safety.

Doe v. Sparks, 733 F. Supp. 227 (W.D. Pa. 1990)—Declaring a prison's policy of denying visitation with same-sex partners constitutionally invalid.

Outing Inmates as LGBTI or HIV Positive

Powell v. Shriver, 175 F.3d 107 (2d Cir. 1999)—Finding that guards who disclosed an inmate's transsexual status were deliberately indifferent to the inmate's safety.

Thomas v. District of Columbia, 887 F. Supp. 1 (D.D.C. 1995)—Holding that an inmate could sustain an Eighth Amendment claim against a guard who spread a rumor that the inmate was homosexual.

Sterling v. Borough of Minersville, 232 F.3d 190 (3d Cir. 2000)—"[O]fficer's threat to disclose arrestee's suspected homosexuality violated arrestee's constitutional right to privacy."

Allowable Gender-Nonconforming Grooming Practices for Transgender Inmates

Lamb v. Maschner, 633 F. Supp. 351 (D. Kan. 1986)—Holding that an inmate did not have a constitutional right to receive cosmetics and female clothing.

Cole v. Flick, 758 F.2d 124 (3d Cir. 1985)—Stating that the prison officials' belief in a correlation between long hair and predatory homosexuals was unreasonable.

Pollock v. Marshall, 845 F.2d 656 (6th Cir. 1988)—Upholding a prison regulation requiring short haircuts based on the prison's legitimate penological interests of "quick identification, removal of place to hide small contraband, prevention of sanitation problems, and homosexual attacks."

Resources

Publications—General and Adult

American Bar Association. 2010. *ABA Standards for Criminal Justice on the Treatment of Prisoners*, 3rd ed. Washington, DC: American Bar Association, *http://www.americanbar.org/content/dam/aba/publications/criminal_justice_ standards/Treatment_of_Prisoners.authcheckdam.pdf*, accessed April 22, 2013.

> Any examination of a transgender person to determine that person's genital status should be performed in private by a qualified medical professional, and only if the person's genital status is unknown to the correctional agency.

American Medical Association House of Delegates. 2008. "Resolution 122: Removing Financial Barriers to Care for Transgender Patients," *http://www.tgender.net/taw/ama_resolutions.pdf*, accessed April 19, 2013.

> Resolution supporting health insurance coverage for treatment of gender identity disorder.

American Medical Association House of Delegates. 2000. "Resolution 506: Policy Statement on Sexual Orientation Reparative (Conversion) Therapy," *http://www.ama-assn.org/resources/doc/mss/mss-proceedings-all.pdf*, accessed April 19, 2013.

> Resolution opposing conversion therapy designed to change sexual orientation.

American Psychiatric Association. 2000. *Diagnostic and Statistical Manual of Mental Disorders, Fourth Edition, Text Revision* (DSM-IV-TR). Arlington, VA: American Psychiatric Association.

> Classification and description of mental disorders.

American Psychiatric Association. August 16, 2012. "APA Issues Official Positions Supporting Access to Care and the Rights of Transgender and Gender Variant Persons," *http://alert.psychiatricnews.org/2012/08/apa-issues-official-positions.html*, accessed April 19, 2013.

> Position statement on appropriate care for transgender people.

American Psychiatric Association. "LGBT – Sexual Orientation," *http://www.psychiatry.org/mental-health/people/lgbt-sexual-orientation*, accessed April 19, 2013.

> Guide on sexual orientation, coming out, and stigma based on sexual orientation.

American Psychoanalytic Association. 2006. "Position Statement: Reparative Therapy," *http://www.apsa.org/about_ apsaa/position_statements/reparativetherapy/tabid/472/default.aspx*, accessed August 5, 2009.

> Position statement that psychoanalytic techniques do not include attempts to "convert" or "repair" an individual's sexual orientation.

American Psychological Association. "Answers to Your Questions: For a Better Understanding of Sexual Orientation & Homosexuality," *http://www.apa.org/topics/sexuality/sorientation.pdf,* accessed April 19, 2013.

Guide that answers common questions about sexual orientation, coming out, and same-sex relationships.

American Psychological Association "Sexual Orientation and Homosexuality," *http://www.apa.org/helpcenter/sexual-orientation.aspx,* accessed April 19, 2013.

The American Psychological Association has recognized that prejudice and discrimination against individuals who have identified as LGBTI tend to result in negative psychological effects. In response, the American Psychological Association wrote a guide to provide information to help people better understand sexual orientation and the harmful impact of prejudice and discrimination.

American Psychological Association Policy Statement. August 2008. "Transgender, Gender Identity, and Gender Expression Non-Discrimination," *http://www.apa.org/about/policy/transgender.aspx,* accessed April 19, 2013.

The American Psychological Association issued this policy statement in support of protecting the rights, legal benefits, and privileges of transgender men and women. The American Psychological Association supports the legal and social recognition of transgender individuals, and encourages psychologists to not only provide treatment but to work against discrimination.

American Psychological Association. August 2009. *Report of the American Psychological Association Task Force on Appropriate Therapeutic Responses to Sexual Orientation, http://www.apa.org/pi/lgbt/resources/therapeutic-response.pdf.*

The American Psychological Association Task Force reviewed literature and studies on sexual orientation change efforts and ultimately found that efforts to change sexual orientation are not successful and can actually cause harm. If a patient seeks sexual orientation change efforts, the American Psychological Association recommends providing care without seeking a specific sexual orientation identity outcome.

Association for Lesbian, Gay, Bisexual, and Transgender Issues in Counseling. 2009. *Competencies for Counseling with Transgender Clients.* Alexandria, VA, *http://www.counseling.org/Resources/Competencies/ALGBTIC_Competencies.pdf,* accessed April 23, 2013.

Guidelines for counseling transgender clients.

Beck, A., and P. Harrison. 2008. *Sexual Victimization in Local Jails Reported by Inmates, 2007.* Washington, DC: U.S. Department of Justice, Bureau of Justice Statistics, *http://bjs.ojp.usdoj.gov/content/pub/pdf/svljri07.pdf,* accessed April 19, 2013.

A report on the findings of a 2007 study examining incidents of sexual victimization amongst 40,419 inmates in 282 local jails. The study found inmates who reported a sexual orientation other than heterosexual were at a significantly higher risk for sexual victimization. 18.5% of homosexual inmates and 9.8% of bisexual inmates, or inmates indicating "other" as sexual orientation, reported an incident of sexual victimization, as compared with only 2.7% of heterosexual inmates.

Bockting, Walter O., and Eli Coleman, 1992. "A Comprehensive Approach to the Treatment of Gender Dysphoria." In Walter O. Bockting and Eli Coleman (eds.), *Interdisciplinary Approaches in Clinical Management.* Binghamton, NY: Haworth Press, p. 131.

Book chapter presenting a new treatment model for those with gender dysphoria. The treatment model's focus is on assessment, management of psychiatric disorders, identity formation and management, and aftercare.

Brown, George R. 2007. "Transvestism and Gender Identity Disorder in Adults." In Glen O. Gabbard (ed.), *Gabbard's Treatments of Psychiatric Disorders*, 3rd ed. Washington, DC: American Psychiatric Press, Inc.

Cole, Collier M., Michael O'Boyle, Lee E. Emory, and Walther J. Meyer III. 1997. "Comorbidity of Gender Dysphoria and Other Major Psychiatric Diagnoses," *Archives of Sexual Behavior* 26, 1:13-26.

A study finding that individuals suffering from gender dysphoria do not suffer from coexisting psychiatric illnesses (such as schizophrenia or major depression) at significantly higher rates than the general population.

Columbia Human Rights Law Review. 2009. "A Jailhouse Lawyer's Manual, Special Information for Lesbian, Gay, Bisexual, and Transgender People, 8th ed. Columbia Human Rights Law Review, *http://www3.law.columbia.edu/hrlr/ JLM/Chapter_30.pdf*, accessed April 23, 2013.

Gives an overview of several resources and remedies for LGBT people and discusses Supreme Court cases and prison regulations such as: right to control gender identity; the right to medical care, including hormone treatment; confidentiality; protective custody and housing; visitation rights; and right to receive LGBT literature.

Gay and Lesbian Advocates and Defenders. 2012. Resources for Prisoners and Ex-Offenders in New England, *http:// www.glad.org/uploads/docs/publications/resources-for-people-and-ex-offenders-in-ne.pdf*, accessed April 23, 2013.

State-by-state resource guide for current and former inmates in New England.

Grant, Jaime M., Lisa A. Moffet, and Justin Tanis. 2011. *Injustice at Every Turn: A Report of the National Transgender Discrimination Survey*. Washington, DC: National Center for Transgender Equality and National Gay and Lesbian Task Force, *http://www.thetaskforce.org/downloads/reports/reports/ntds_full.pdf*, accessed April 22, 2013.

Survey of 6,450 transgender and gender-nonconforming individuals reporting incidents of discrimination based on gender identity.

The Harry Benjamin International Gender Dysphoria Association's Standards Of Care For Gender Identity Disorders, Sixth Version. 2001. *http://www.wpath.org/documents2/socv6.pdf*, accessed April 22, 2013.

Standards for the treatment and care of those with gender dysphoria.

Herek, Gregory M. "Facts About Homosexuality and Child Molestation," *http://psychology.ucdavis.edu/rainbow/html/ facts_molestation.html*, accessed April 22, 2013.

Fact sheet discrediting the stereotype that LGBT individuals are a special danger to children.

Herek, Gregory M., and Linda D. Garnets. 2007. "Sexual Orientation and Mental Health." *Annual Review of Clinical Psychology* 3, 353.

Article discussing mental health and sexual orientation. The article summarizes psychological research and shares the findings about mental well-being and distress among nonheterosexuals, examining the stressors that are unique to sexual minorities.

Israel, Gianna E., and Donald E. Tarver II. 1997. *Transgender Care: Recommended Guidelines, Practical Information, and Personal Accounts.* Philadelphia, PA: Temple University Press.

Guidelines which provide a framework for addressing transgender issues, including gender-appropriate pronouns. Suggests creating a new specialty, the "gender specialist," to provide psychotherapy, counseling, and education about gender identity.

Jenness, Valerie, Cheryl L. Maxson, Kristy N. Matsuda, and Jennifer Macy Sumner. 2007. *Violence in California Correctional Facilities: An Empirical Examination of Sexual Assault.* Center for Evidence-Based Corrections, University of California, Irvine.

Presentation of the findings of a study regarding sexual abuse in six California prisons. The study aimed to examine the extent and nature of sexual assault within the correctional facilities. The study reported several findings in the areas of the prevalence of sexual assault, characteristics of the victims, and characteristics of the incidents.

Jenny, Carole, Thomas A. Roesler, and Kimberly L. Poyer. 1994. "Are Children at Risk for Sexual Abuse by Homosexuals?" *Pediatrics* 94, 1: 41-44.

This study was conducted in response to anti-gay legislation that had passed in several states, limiting placements in jobs with access to children. The study looked at incidents of abuse of a group of children over the course of a year, and found that the likelihood of a child being abused by a gay or lesbian individual was minimal.

Just Detention International. 2009. "A Call for Change: Protecting the Rights of LGBTQ Detainees," *http://www.justdetention.org/pdf/CFCLGBTQJan09.pdf,* accessed April 22, 2013.

Discussion of PREA standards regarding prisoner awareness, promoting safety, staff screening and training, responding to sexual violence, and monitoring.

Leach, Donald L. 2007. *Managing Lesbian, Gay, Bisexual, Transgender, and Intersex Inmates: Is Your Jail Ready?* Washington, DC: U.S. Department of Justice, National Institute of Corrections, *http://community.nicic.gov/blogs/national_jail_exchange/archive/2011/01/25/managing-lesbian-gay-bisexual-transgender-and-intersex-inmates-is-your-jail-ready.aspx,* accessed April 22, 2013.

Provides a list of questions jails must consider with regard to medical care, data systems, housing, security, and clothing for LGBTI people.

Lucas, Kimberley D., Jamie L. Miller, Valorie Eckert, Stacy Goldsby, Megan C. Henry, Michael C. Samuel, and Janet C. Mohle-Boetani. 2011. *Evaluation of a Prisoner Condom Access Pilot Program Conducted in One California State Prison Facility.* Public Health Unit: California Correction Health Care Services, *http://www.cdph.ca.gov/programs/std/Documents/SBD%20Pilot_Final%20Report_122210-CDPH-CCHCS_September2011.pdf,* accessed April 24, 2013.

Study examining the feasibility of providing condoms to inmates.

McConaghy, Nathaniel. 1998. "Paedophelia: A Review of the Evidence." *Australian & New Zealand Journal of Psychiatry* 32, 2: 252.

Study examining literature from the previous 30 years concerning the nature and presence of pedophilia.

National Center for Lesbian Rights. 2006. *Rights of Transgender Prisoners, http://www.nclrights.org/site/DocServer/RightsofTransgenderPeople.pdf?docID=6381,* accessed April 23, 2013.

Overview of the rights of transgender people, with regard to housing, inmate violence, and hormone therapy.

National Commission on Correctional Health Care. 2009. "Position Statement: Transgender Health Care in Correctional Settings," *http://www.ncchc.org/transgender-health-care-in-correctional-settings*, accessed April 22, 2013.

Standards relating to health management of transgender inmates.

National Institute of Corrections. "Lesbian, Gay, Bisexual, Transgender and Intersex Inmates," *http://nicic.gov/LGBTI*, accessed April 22, 2013.

Offering limited, short-term technical assistance to agencies that are seeking to examine and improve responses to management of LGBTI inmates.

National Sexual Violence Resource Center. 2009. *National Prison Rape Elimination Commission Report.* Washington, DC: National Prison Rape Elimination Commission, *http://www.nsvrc.org/publications/reports/national-prison-rape-elimination-commission-report*, accessed April 22, 2013.

Detailed report by the National Prison Rape Elimination Commission, providing statistics and personal stories of inmates who are sexually abused while in custody.

The National Victim Center and The Crime Victims Research and Treatment Center. 1992. *Rape in America: A Report to the Nation.* Arlington, VA, *http://www.musc.edu/ncvc/resources_prof/rape_in_america.pdf*, accessed April 22, 2013.

Report compiling statistics on rapes committed across the United States.

Raising the Bar for Justice & Safety Coalition, *http://raisingthebarcoalition.org*, accessed April 22, 2013.

News and information regarding the PREA standards, including transgender and intersex inmates search recommendations.

Sexton, Lori, Valerie Jenness, and Jennifer Macy Sumner. 2010. "Where the Margins Meet: A Demographic Assessment of Transgender Inmates in Men's Prisons." *Justice Quarterly* 27: 6.

A report providing a profile of transgender prisoners.

Stop Prisoner Rape. 2006. *In the Shadows: Sexual Violence in US Detention Facilities.* Los Angeles, CA: Stop Prisoner Rape, *http://www.justdetention.org/pdf/in_the_shadows.pdf*, accessed April 22, 2013.

Report developed by Stop Prisoner Rape (SPR) for the United Nations Committee Against Torture. The report highlights the sexual abuse of men, women, and youth in detention facilities and offers recommendations to stop the abuse. Among the recommendations are holding those who commit sexual abuse to be responsible for their crimes, reducing overcrowding, protecting "at-risk groups," and providing mental and physical health care after abuse occurs.

Stop Prisoner Rape ACLU National Prison Project. 2005. *Still in Danger: The Ongoing Threat of Sexual Violence Against Transgender Prisoners.* Los Angeles, CA: Stop Prisoner Rape, *http://www.justdetention.org/pdf/stillindanger.pdf*, accessed April 22, 2013.

Report reviewing the legal implications of the Supreme Court's decision in *Farmer* v. *Brennan* regarding Eighth Amendment claims and providing an assessment of changes in conditions for transgender prisoners since the decision. The report gives recommendations on the treatment of transgender prisoners, including alternative housing assignments to isolation, allowing choice in gender of officer conducting pat-down searches, and respecting objections to roommate assignments due to fear of abuse.

Struckman-Johnson, C., and D. Struckman-Johnson. 2006. "A Comparison of Sexual Coercion Experiences Reported by Men and Women in Prison," *Journal of Interpersonal Violence* 21, 12: 1591.

Report detailing the responses of 382 men and 51 women across 10 Midwestern prisons who self-reported sexual coercion while incarcerated.

Sumner, Jennifer Macy. 2011. "Keeping House: Understanding the Transgender Inmate Code of Conduct Through Prison Policies, Environments, and Culture," Ph.D. dissertation, University of California, Irvine.

A code of conduct created for corrections facilities, made after interviewing 315 transgender inmates in California prisons.

Sylla, Mary. 2008. "Access to Condoms in the United States – The Challenge of Introducing Harm Reduction into a Law and Order Environment." Paper presented at the Project UNSHACKLE meeting, The John M. Lloyd AIDS Project at Stony Point Center, May 16-18, 2008.

Outlining three successful condom access programs in correctional facilities:

- San Francisco, Forensic AIDS Project: Installed a condom machine in the prison gymnasium and allows each person to take one condom per week.

- Philadelphia: People are able get condoms through the nurse or by purchase at the commissary. Each person is allowed to be in possession of six condoms at a time. Anecdotal evidence suggests few condoms are purchased at the commissary.

- Los Angeles: Each segregated, gay male person can receive one condom per week, distributed by a Center for Health Justice staff member.

Sylvia Rivera Law Project. 2007. *"It's war in here": A Report on the Treatment of Transgender and Intersex People in New York State Men's Prisons*, http://srlp.org/wp-content/uploads/2012/08/WarinHere042007.pdf, accessed April 22, 2013.

Report outlining the experiences of transgender, gender-nonconforming, and intersex people in New York State men's prisons. The researchers conducted interviews with 12 current and former inmates and 10 advocates to testify to their experiences in the system and working within the system.

United Nations Office on Drugs and Crime. 2009. *Handbook on Prisoners with Special Needs.* New York: United Nations, http://www.unodc.org/pdf/criminal_justice/Handbook_on_People_with_Special_Needs.pdf, accessed April 22, 2013.

Makes recommendations for the care and treatment of LGBTI inmates in terms of staffing, housing, visitation, health care, safety, and monitoring.

U.S. Customs and Immigration Enforcement. 2011. *Performance-Based National Detention Standards 2011*, http://www.ice.gov/doclib/detention-standards/2011/pbnds2011.pdf, accessed April 23, 2013.

Provides guidelines for handling transgender people in immigration detention centers.

U.S. Federal Register. 2012. *National Standards to Prevent, Detect, and Respond to Prison Rape, 28 C.F.R. 115, https://www.federalregister.gov/articles/2012/06/20/2012-12427/national-standards-to-prevent-detect-and-respond-to-prison-rape*, accessed April 22, 2013.

> Final standards for the prevention and detection of prison rape.

Whitman, Joy S., Harriet L. Glosoff, Michael M. Kocet, and Vilia Tarvydas. 2006. "Exploring ethical issues related to conversion or reparative therapy," *http://ct.counseling.org/2006/05/exploring-ethical-issues-related-to-conversion-or-reparative-therapy*, accessed April 22, 2013.

> American Counseling Association does not endorse conversion therapy and provides guidelines for handling patients who express an interest in receiving such therapy.

Wilkinson, Willy. "Best Practices for Serving Lesbian, Gay, Bisexual, and Transgendered Individuals in Women's Treatment Settings," *http://ontrackconsulting.org/docs/lgbt-best-practices.pdf*, accessed April 22, 2013.

> Provides ideas and suggestions for developing policies to create a nondiscriminatory environment in women's treatment settings.

Wolfe, Zachary. "Gay and Lesbian Prisoners: Recent Developments and a Call for More Research." *Prison Legal News, https://www.prisonlegalnews.org/displayArticle.aspx?articleid=20578&AspxAutoDetectCookieSupport=1*, accessed April 23, 2013.

> Calling for enhanced equality in spousal visitation, right to receive information, and highlighting of the harmful effects of segregation.

Publications—Youth

American Academy of Child & Adolescent Psychiatry. January 2006. "Facts for Families: Gay, Lesbian and Bisexual Adolescents," *http://www.aacap.org/page.ww?section=Facts%20for%20Families&name=Gay,%20Lesbian%20and%20Bisexual%20Adolescents*, accessed August 5, 2009.

> Tips for parents on understanding their LGBT child, including an overview of difficulties facing LGBT adolescents.

Beck, A., P. Harrison, and P. Guerino. 2010. *Sexual Victimization in Juvenile Facilities Reported by Youth, 2008-09*, Washington, DC: U.S. Department of Justice, Bureau of Justice Statistics, *http://bjs.ojp.usdoj.gov/content/pub/pdf/svjfry09.pdf*, accessed April 19, 2013.

> A report on the findings of the National Survey of Youth in Custody (NSYC), mandated by the Prison Rape Elimination Act. The report includes incidents of sexual abuse reported by LGBT inmates.

Boland, Patricia. 2008. "Vulnerability to Violence Among Gay, Lesbian and Bisexual Youth." NASP Resources, *http://www.nasponline.org/resources/crisis_safety/neat_vulnerability.aspx*, accessed April 22, 2013.

> Article describing developmental patterns of gender-variant children and the ways in which LGBT youth are victimized. This article provides suggestions for schools and school psychologists to better assist gender-variant children.

Brill, Stephanie, and Rachel Pepper. 2008. *The Transgender Child: A Handbook for Families and Professionals.* San Francisco, CA: Cleis Press, Inc., pp. 16-17.

> Guidebook to assist families in understanding their gender-variant or transgender child. Discusses topics such as acceptance of transgender children, developmental stages and transition periods, and effective parenting practices.

Cathcart, Rebecca. 2008. "Boy's Killing, Labeled a Hate Crime, Stuns Town." *New York Times, http://www.nytimes. com/2008/02/23/us/23oxnard.html?_r=0*, accessed April 22, 2013.

> Recounting the story of a young boy killed at school, purportedly due to his sexual orientation.

DeCrescenzo, Teresa, and Gerald P. Mallon. 2002. *Serving Transgender Youth: The Role of the Child Welfare System.* Washington, DC: Child Welfare League of America.

> A report on a roundtable of professionals and transgender youth convened by The Child Welfare League of America to discuss experiences of transgender youth and provide recommendations for child welfare organizations working with transgender youth.

Earls, Meg. July 2005. "Fact Sheet: GLBTQ Youth," *Advocates for Youth, http://www.advocatesforyouth.org/storage/ advfy/documents/fsglbt.pdf,* accessed April 22, 2013.

> Fact sheet concerning the serious issues LGBTQ youth face, including mental and physical health.

Earls, Meg. 2002. "Stressors in the Lives of GLBTQ Youth." *Transitions: Working with GLBTQ Youth* 14, 4, *http:// www.advocatesforyouth.org/publications/publications-a-z/697?task=view,* accessed April 22, 2013.

> Journal article on rejection and societal issues relevant to LGBTIQ youth.

Frankowiski, Barbara L. 2004. "Sexual Orientation and Adolescents," *Pediatrics* 113, 6: 1827-1832, *http://pediatrics. aappublications.org/cgi/reprint/113/6/1827,* accessed April 19, 2013.

> Guide for pediatricians to aid them in understanding the special needs of LGBT youths. The guide encourages pediatricians to provide a supportive environment and provide comprehensive health care, including information about sexual orientation.

Gay & Lesbian Advocates & Defenders. 2013. *Transgender Legal Issues.* Boston, MA: GLAD, *http://www.glad.org/ uploads/docs/publications/trans-legal-issues.pdf,* accessed April 23, 2013.

> Overview of rights of transgender inmates in prisons, including classification, protection from violence, and medical treatment.

Goldman, Linda. 2008. *Coming Out, Coming In: Nurturing the Well-Being and Inclusion of Gay Youth in Mainstream Society.* New York: Routledge.

> A book aimed at providing parents, school administrators, community groups, and counselors with information to provide safe environments for LGBT youth. The book includes information, exercises, anecdotes, and additional resources.

Kruks, Gabe. 1991. "Gay and lesbian homeless/street youth: Special issues and concerns." *Journal of Adolescent Health* 12, 7: 515-518.

Report compiling data on homeless and runaway youth. The report found that gay and bisexual male youth are at an increased risk for homelessness, suicide, and engaging in survival sex.

Los Angeles County Probation Department. July 2008. "Your Handbook of Rules and Rights," *http://probation.co.la.ca.us,* accessed April 22, 2013.

Pamphlet outlining the rights and responsibilities of prisoners in the Los Angeles County Juvenile Hall.

Majd, Katayoon, Jody Marksamer, and Carolyn Reyes. 2009. *Hidden Injustice: Lesbian, Gay, Bisexual and Transgender Youth in Juvenile Courts.* Legal Services for Children, National Juvenile Defender Center, and National Center for Lesbian Rights. San Francisco, CA: Autumn Press, *http://www.equityproject.org/pdfs/hidden_injustice.pdf*, accessed April 22, 2013.

Joint report highlighting the failures of juvenile justice courts to treat LGBT youth fairly, and discusses the current barriers to fair treatment and how to overcome them.

Mallon, Gerald P. 1999. "Practice with Transgendered Children." In *Social Services with Transgendered Youth,* Binghamton, NY: The Haworth Press, pp. 49, 55-56.

Chapter examining gender-variant child development and how gender-variant children recognize and deal with gender identity. The chapter provides recommendations for social workers working with gender-variant children.

Mallon, Gerald P., and Teresa DeCrescenzo. 2006. "Transgender Children and Youth: A Child Welfare Practice Perspective," *Child Welfare Journal* 85, 2: 215-241.

Article that builds upon and updates the analysis of gender-variant child development begun in *Practice with Transgendered Children.*

Marksamer, Jody. 2011. *A Place of Respect: A Guide for Group Care Facilities Serving Transgender and Gender Non-Conforming Youth.* San Francisco, CA: National Center for Lesbian Rights, *http://www.nclrights.org/site/DocServer/A_Place_Of_Respect.pdf?docID=8301*, accessed April 23, 2013.

Guide for youth group care facility staff to provide transgender and gender-nonconforming youth with appropriate care.

National Center for Juvenile Justice. 2002. *Desktop Guide to Good Juvenile Probation Practice, Revised.* Patricia Torbet and Patrick Griffin (eds.). Pittsburgh, PA: National Council of Juvenile and Family Court Judges.

Collection of best practices for juvenile probation departments.

National Center for Lesbian Rights. 2006. *The Legal Rights of Lesbian, Gay, Bisexual, and Transgender Youth in the Juvenile Justice System.* San Francisco, CA: NCLR, *http://www.equityproject.org/pdfs/Legal_Rights_LGBTQYouth_Juvenile_Justice.pdf*, accessed April 23, 2013.

Overview of rights of LGBTI youth to not be isolated, to be free from sex offender label, to receive appropriate health and mental care, to be free from discrimination, to express sexual orientation and gender identity, and not to participate in religious activities.

National Coalition for the Homeless. 2008. "Homeless Youth," *http://nationalhomeless.org/factsheets/youth.html*, accessed April 22, 2013.

Fact sheet providing the causes and consequences of homelessness among youth.

National Institute of Justice. 1995. *Research Preview: Childhood Victimization and Risk for Alcohol and Drug Arrests.* Washington, DC: U.S. Department of Justice.

A study finding that childhood maltreatment is a significant predictor of adult arrests for alcohol and/or drug-related offenses, but not juvenile offenses.

National Partnership for Juvenile Services. 2012. "Code of Ethics," *http://npjs.org/wp-content/uploads/2013/01/NPJS-Code-of-Ethics.pdf*, accessed April 22, 2013.

Code of ethics for the National Partnership for Juvenile Services.

National Prison Rape Elimination Commission. 2009. *Standards for the Prevention, Detection, Response, and Monitoring of Sexual Abuse in Juvenile Facilities.* Washington, DC, *http://www.wcl.american.edu/endsilence/documents/NPREC_JuvenileStandards.pdf,* accessed April 22, 2013.

Recommendations from the National Prison Rape Elimination Commission for juveniles.

Robert F. Kennedy Center for Justice and Human Rights and New York State United Teachers. 2010. *Speak Truth to Power.* Washington, DC: RFK Center, *http://locals.nysut.org/speaktruth_curriculum_complete.pdf*, accessed April 22, 2013.

Curriculum to combat bullying of various types in schools.

Ryan, Caitlin. 2003. "Lesbian, Gay, Bisexual and Transgender Youth: Health Concerns, Services and Care," *Clinical Research & Regulatory Affairs* 20, 2: 137.

Providing suggestions for schools to develop policies and trainings to better deal with LGBT youth, identity development, and sexual orientation. The guide highlights health and mental concerns for LGBT youth, including HIV infection, victimization, suicide, and substance abuse, and emphasizes ways to create a safe environment and provide appropriate care.

Ryan, Caitlin, and Rafael M. Diaz. 2005. "Family Responses as a Source of Risk and Resiliency for LGBT Youth." Presented at the preconference Institute on LGBTQ Youth, Child Welfare League of America 2005 National Conference, Washington, DC.

Report on the experiences of LGBT youth in the child welfare system. The report outlines the attitudes towards LGBT youth in the foster care and adoption systems, and encourages the creation of safe and supportive placements.

Ryan, Caitlin, and Donna Futterman. 1998. *Lesbian & Gay Youth: Care & Counseling.* New York: Columbia University Press.

Book providing an overview of the needs and experiences of LGBT youth, theorizing that it is stigma which sets LGBT youth apart from their peers. The book provides recommendation for prevention and primary care for health and mental concerns of LGBT adolescents.

Savin-Williams, Ritch C. 1994. "Verbal and Physical Abuse as Stressors in the Lives of Lesbian, Gay Male, and Bisexual Youths: Associations with School Problems, Running Away, Substance Abuse, Prostitution, and Suicide." *Journal of Consulting and Clinical Psychology* 62: 261.

A review of the verbal and physical abuse experienced by LGBT youth and their responses to these stressors. The report found the responses to verbal and physical abuse often included school-related problems, running away from home, legal issues, substance abuse, prostitution, and suicide. The report does not scientifically verify the causal link between the stressors and the responses, but suggests that the responses are in fact the consequences of verbal and physical abuse that LGBT youth suffer.

U.S. Department of Education. 2010. *Key Policy Letters from the Education Secretary and Deputy Secretary.* Washington, DC, *http://www2.ed.gov/policy/gen/guid/secletter/101215.html*, accessed April 22, 2013.

Guidance from the U.S. Department of Education on the best practices to prevent bullying and peer violence in schools.

Wilber, Shannan, Caitlin Ryan, and Jody Marksamer. 2006. *Serving LGBT Youth in Out-of-Home Care: CWLA Best Practice Guidelines,* Washington, DC: Child Welfare League of America, *http://www.lsc-sf.org/wp-content/uploads/bestpracticeslgbtyouth.pdf,* accessed April 23, 2013.

Compilation of guidelines for out-of-home care for LGBTI youth.

Web Sites

Bureau of Justice Statistics
http://bjs.gov/index.cfm?ty=dcdetail&iid=406

The Center for HIV Law & Policy
http://hivlawandpolicy.org/resources/view/539

The Equity Project
http://equityproject.org/

Federal Bureau of Investigation
http://www.fbi.gov/about-us/investigate/civilrights/hate_crimes/hate_crimes

Intersex Society of North America
http://www.isna.org/

National Institute of Corrections
http://nicic.gov/LGBTI

Prison Library Project
http://prisonlibraryproject.org

TGI Justice: Transgender Gender Variant Intersex Justice
http://www.tgijp.org/

Transgender Law and Policy Institute
http://www.transgenderlaw.org/index.htm

The White House
http://www.whitehouse.gov/lgbt

Sample Policies

Following are examples of policies that agencies are using to address the needs of LGBTI adults and youth in custody. These are not "model" policies and only represent the approaches of the particular agencies.

Jail

Denver Sheriff Department. 2012. "Transgender and Gender-Variant Inmates," *http://thecrimereport.s3.amazonaws. com/2/28/d/1701/gray_transgender_prison_rape_pdf_attachment.pdf*, accessed April 23, 2013.

Prison

California Department of Corrections and Rehabilitation. 2013. *Department Operations Manual, http://www.cdcr. ca.gov/Regulations/Adult_Operations/DOM_TOC.html*, accessed April 24, 2013.

District of Columbia Department of Corrections. 2011. "Gender Classification and Housing," No. 4020.3C, *http://doc. dc.gov/sites/default/files/dc/sites/doc/publication/attachments/DOC_PS_4020_3C_Gender_Classificationand_ Housing_01112012_wsig.pdf*, accessed April 24, 2013.

Hawaii Department of Public Safety. 2007. "Medical Treatment For Transsexual Inmates," No. COR.10.1E.16, *http://dps. hawaii.gov/wp-content/uploads/2012/10/COR.10.1E.16.pdf*, accessed April 24, 2013.

Massachusetts Department of Correction. 2010. "Identification, Treatment and Correctional Management of Inmates Diagnosed with Gender Identity Disorder (GID)," No. 103 DOC 652, *http://www.mass.gov/eopss/docs/doc/ policies/652.pdf*, accessed April 24, 2013.

Michigan Department of Corrections. 2010. "Gender Identity Disorders in Prisoners," No. 04.06.184, *http://www. michigan.gov/documents/corrections/0406184_340784_7.pdf*, accessed April 24, 2013.

Minnesota Department of Corrections. 2007. "Evaluation and Placement of Transgender Offenders," No. 202.045, *http://www.doc.state.mn.us/DocPolicy2/html/DPW_Display_TOC.asp?Opt=202.045.htm*, accessed April 24, 2013.

Ohio Department of Rehabilitation and Correction. 2013. "Medical Legal Issues," No. 68-MED-09, *http://www.drc.ohio. gov/web/drc_policies/documents/68-MED-09.pdf*, accessed April 24, 2013.

Washington State Department of Corrections. 2012. "Health Services Management," No. DOC 600.000, *http://www. doc.wa.gov/Policies/default.aspx?show=600*, accessed April 24, 2013.

Juvenile

Alameda County Social Services Agency. 2007. "Department of Children and Family Services LGBTQ Policy," *http:// pathwaytohome.org/adoption/LGBTQPolicyFinalapproved3-6-07.pdf*, accessed April 24, 2013.

State of Connecticut Policy Manual. 2004. "Non-Discrimination of LGBTQI Individuals," No. 30-9, *http://www.ncsl.org/ print/cyf/Connecticut_CYF_Policy.pdf*, accessed April 24, 2013.

State of Illinois Department of Children and Family Services. 2002. "Assessment and Treatment of Lesbian, Gay, Bisexual, Transgender and Questioning (LGBTQ) Youths," No. 2002.17, *http://www.state.il.us/dcfs/docs/ocfp/policy/ pg200217.pdf,* accessed April 24, 2013.

New York State Office of Children and Family Services. 2008. "Lesbian, Gay, Bisexual, Transgender and Questioning Youth," No. PPM 3442.00, *http://archive.srlp.org/files/LGBTQ_Youth_Policy_PPM_3442_00.pdf,* accessed April 24, 2013.

Appendix E

Training Matrix

This appendix contains resources (a matrix of topics for staff and youth) for training and curricula development on addressing the needs of LGBTI adults and youth in custody.

Recommended Training for Staff

SUBJECT	AUDIENCE						
	ADMIN. AND LEGAL	LINE STAFF	INVESTIGATIONS AND HR	MEDICAL AND MENTAL HEALTH STAFF	JUVENILE STAFF	VOLUNTEERS	CONTRACTORS
Understanding LGBTI Inmates/Youth	X	X	X	X	X	X	X
Definitions and terminology							
Special concerns and unique needs							
Addressing myths about LGBTI inmates/youth							
Effective interventions: harassment							
Prison Rape Elimination Act	X	X	X	X	X	X	X
Human Development and Sexuality	X	X	X	X	X	X	X
Why understanding sexuality in this context is important							
Development and gender identity							
Culture	X	X	X	X	X	X	X
Role of leadership							
Staff attitudes							
The code of silence							
Staff who identify as LGBTI							
State Laws	X	X	X	X	X	X	X
Agency Policy	X	X	X	X	X	X	X
Operational Practices	X						
Classification							
Searches							
Supervision of LGBTI offenders/youth							

	AUDIENCE						
SUBJECT	ADMIN. AND LEGAL	LINE STAFF	INVESTIGATIONS AND HR	MEDICAL AND MENTAL HEALTH STAFF	JUVENILE STAFF	VOLUNTEERS	CONTRACTORS
Medical and Mental Health Care	X			X			
Treatment protocols							
Managing Vulnerable Inmates	X	X	X	X	X	X	X
Risks for LGBTI inmates/youth							
Human Resource Issues	X		X				
Unions							
Collective bargaining							
Civil Liability	X	X	X	X	X	X	X

Recommended Training for Youth

	AUDIENCE			
SUBJECT	BOYS 10–15	BOYS 16–19	GIRLS 10–15	GIRLS 16–19
Understanding LGBTI Youth	X	X	X	X
Definitions and terminology				
Addressing myths about LGBTI inmates/youth				
Effective interventions: harassment				
Commitment to Safety	X	X	X	X
Agency values				
Available resources				
What to expect				
Agency policy				
Adolescent Development and Sexuality	Only some portions of this section	X	Only some portions of this section	X
Appropriate activities				
Healthy boundaries				
Appropriate relationships				
Sexually transmitted diseases				
Healthy choices				
LGBTIQQ				
Sexual arousal (what to do)				
Physical				
Emotional				
Cognitive				
Gender differences				
Hygiene				

	AUDIENCE			
SUBJECT	BOYS 10–15	BOYS 16–19	GIRLS 10–15	GIRLS 16–19
Culture Adolescent culture Agency culture Bullying Red flags Religious beliefs Values Terminology/communication Drugs Diversity	Only some portions of this section	X	Only some portions of this section	X
Victimization Prevention Past victimization Protecting oneself Medical treatment	X	X	X	X